Understanding Organizational Leadership through Ubuntu

By

Chiku Malunga

Published by
Adonis & Abbey Publishers Ltd
P.O. Box 43418
London
SE11 4XZ
http://www.adonis-abbey.com
Email: editor@adonis-abbey.com

First Edition, 2009

British Library Cataloguing-in-Publication Data

A catalogue record for this book is available from the British Library.

ISBN: 9781906704490(HB)/9781906704490

Printed and bound in Great Britain.

Understanding Organizational Leadership through Ubuntu

By

Chiku Malunga

ACKNOWLEDGEMENTS

I owe thanks to many people and organizations whose support made the writing of this book possible. First I must acknowledge INTRAC for offering me a fellowship that helped me to concentrate on the fine details of the book in Oxford. I want to thank the leaders of the organizations I interviewed for the research. I also want to thank all the organizations I have worked with in the capacity of a consultant or adviser in Africa, Europe and America. These have been my real classroom where I have learnt organization development and leadership as they really work on the ground. I want to thank my two mentors Professor Alan Fowler and Professor Gomo Michongwe for helping me discover my voice and my place as an author.

Professor John Hailey, Rick James, Jeff Kwaterski and Pastor Pangani Thipa: thanks so much for the professional and personal support rendered throughout the project.

I want to recognize the Spirit. Thanks for occasionally waking me up in the middle of the night with insights in the form of the still small voice to give the content of the book a freshness that would not be possible otherwise. Writing this book over a period of four years has been more of a journey of self-discovery and some sort of a spiritual awakening.

Most important, I want to thank my wife Chawanangwa who, as President Obama would say, is the love of my life, for her continued understanding and patience throughout this project and all the other projects.

Kampala, Uganda 24 April, 2009
Chiku Malunga

Dedication

I dedicate this book to my two daughters, Thandi and Tia. I believe that the wisdom upon which it is based will contribute towards a wiser and more sustainable world in which they will have to live.

Table of Contents

INTRODUCTION

There is an imaginary story about the great flood talked about in the Bible. The story goes something like this. Before God went to Noah to ask him to build an ark in preparation for the rain, he went to his brother. Noah's brother, basing himself on his concept of rain, told God that he did not need to build an ark in preparation for the rain. He said he would simply buy some buckets to capture the rainwater as it fell. The rain he had seen all his life was managed by simply collecting the rainwater in buckets. God, knowing the magnitude of the rain he was talking about, tried to persuade him to build the ark but to no avail. Frustrated, God went to Noah who fortunately did build the ark. The rest is obvious. The point of the story is that organizations and people in general tend to underestimate the magnitude of the challenges they are facing. Their preparation and response often do not match up to the level of the challenge. This is often because we only see the tip of the iceberg. Climate change, environmental degradation, conflict, HIV and AIDS, the global financial crisis and poverty are some of the floods that 'buckets' cannot do much to address.

This book, by taking a particular approach, is aimed at helping organizations and individuals build 'arks' and not to 'buy buckets' in their response to the challenges they are addressing. It is aimed at helping organizations and individuals build a strong and sustainable foundation for success.

In trying to help organizations and individuals 'build arks' and not 'buy buckets', this book is motivated by the need to find more effective ways of communicating organizational issues and addressing them. It is built on the idea that the indigenous wisdom contained in African proverbs can be used to communicate 'modern' organizational issues much more eloquently than most conventional methods. One proverb can explain an organizational aspect much more effectively than an entire chapter in a classic organizational or management textbook. A proverb like *If the sun says it is more powerful than the moon then let it come and shine at night,* for example, demonstrates the importance for those holding senior positions in organizations to recognize and respect the role played by those holding less senior positions more forcefully than is possible with most conventional methods. A proverb like *When a madman slaps you and you slap him back then both of you are mad* teaches the importance of responding with wisdom when provoked by 'lesser and misguided people'. The use of African proverbs therefore offers an opportunity to improve organizational performance in ways that may not be possible with most conventional methods.

The book uses the indigenous wisdom contained in African proverbs to awaken organizational consciousness. While my first book, *Understanding Organizational Sustainability through African Proverbs*, focused on issues of financial and organizational sustainability and was mostly inspirational in nature, and the second book, *Making Strategic Plans Work: Insights from African Indigenous Wisdom*, concentrated on how to improve the practice of strategic planning and strategic management in organizations, this book takes a more holistic view of organizations and offers practical guidance on how to improve organizational performance using the wisdom contained in African proverbs.

What are Proverbs?

Proverbs are an integral part of African culture. They are simple statements with deep meaning. They are guidelines for individual, family and village behaviour, built upon repeated real life experiences and observations over time. Proverbs are a mirror through which people look at themselves – a stage for expressing themselves to others. The way people think and look at the world, their culture, values, behaviours, aspirations and preoccupations can immediately be understood by looking at their proverbs.

Proverbs constitute the words of ancestors and forefathers and foremothers that are passed to grandchildren and great-grandchildren. They teach about respect, strengthen families and extended family relationships, teach people about how to live peacefully with one another and/or good neighbourliness, and above all place an emphasis on personhood or *ubuntu* – the essence of being human. In more practical terms proverbs alert and caution against bad habits and wrongdoing, criminal acts, social problems and bad influences or spitefulness (Mapadimeng, 2007: 259). A proverb like *What business does an egg have dancing with the stones?* can be used to teach innocent children to avoid bad company or associations which may 'break' their good values. While Africa has many languages, proverbs offer them common ground. The same proverbs recur in similar forms in almost all African languages and societies. Some state facts from a people's history, customs and practices; others express philosophical thoughts, beliefs and values. Yet they make communication instantly possible, irrespective of differences in geographic origin and cultural backgrounds. Proverbs are the common property of Africans because they are ascribed to wisdom of all the ancestors.

Use of Proverbs

According to the BBC's *Wisdom of Africa* book, 'proverbs are used to illustrate ideas, reinforce arguments and deliver messages of inspiration, consolation, celebration and advice'. More specifically:

Proverbs identify and dignify a culture. They express the collective wisdom of the people, reflecting their thinking, values and behaviour. Using proverbs to communicate and understand organizational issues is a very powerful tool in the quest for a genuine African identity.

In indigenous Africa, proverbs are used to unlock immobility, clarify vision and unify different perspectives. Proverbs add humour and defuse tension on otherwise very sensitive issues. Every African society has used proverbs for centuries to ease uncomfortable situations, confront issues and build institutions and relationships. They can be understood where literacy is low and yet appreciated by even the most educated.

Proverbs are metaphors and can explain complex issues in simple statements. A proverb like *A stewed liver may look smooth and easy to swallow but it can choke one to death* may be a powerful statement in encouraging people to change their sexual behaviour in the light of HIV and AIDS – i.e. not to be deceived by how somebody looks and assume that they cannot pass on the virus. Proverbs like *When one begs for water it does not quench thirst* and *If you borrow a man's legs, you will go where he directs you* encourage people to be self-reliant, and they can explain with more force the concept of sustainability than other conventional methods. A proverb like *If a mouse is laughing at a cat it means that it is near a hole* can be used to discuss strategy when provoked by a seemingly weaker opponent.

Proverbs are like seeds. They only become 'alive' when they are 'sown'. They are simple statements until applied to real life situations, bringing them to life and expanding their meaning.

By being metaphorical, proverbs create strong mental pictures. This is a great tool for motivating people to action.

The Power of Metaphors

Metaphors and analogies draw relationships of likeness between two things – often very unlike things – and are used for vividness, for clarification, or to explain certain emotions as it is difficult to move people without touching their emotions (Conger, 1998: 78). A metaphor enables a person to visualise the object, and then the person goes through a mental process of deciphering what the message means on a visual, cognitive and emotional level. There is often a moment of puzzlement trying to decode the message; this pause ensures that the listener is both stimulated and concentrating on the speaker's message. In this case, the metaphor presents a paradox. Something that should not be but is. For example, the proverb *Ants united, can carry a dead elephant to their abode.* The ants cannot carry an elephant but in the metaphor they do. It is also a paradox that ends on a positive note. The ants are able to carry the dead elephant to their cave. The reader then interprets the paradox in terms of himself or herself.

Metaphors are most potent when they invoke symbols that have deep cultural roots and, as a result, elicit strong emotions. African proverbs are deeply rooted in African culture. And since the proverbs are not really African but human proverbs, they elicit strong emotions in all people from everywhere.

Gareth Morgan (1997) offers some thoughts on the use of metaphor in organizational improvement efforts. He observes that ideas about organization are always based on implicit images or metaphors that persuade us to see, understand, and manage situations in a particular way. Metaphors create insight but they also distort. They have strengths but they also have limitations. In creating ways of seeing, they create ways of not seeing. Morgan observes that the challenge facing modern managers is therefore to become accomplished in the art of using metaphor to find new ways of seeing, understanding, and shaping their actions. African proverbs as metaphors offer them the opportunity to do this.

The Audience of the Book

This book is about communicating a holistic understanding of organizations in a language that is at the same time humorous and deep enough to motivate people to action. It will be of particular value to organizational leaders and consultants in their organizational performance improvement efforts. Volunteers and expatriates working or coming to work in Africa and other developing regions will learn from the insights in the book how to understand the culture of the people they will be working with better, and therefore how to improve their own relevance and effectiveness. Donor agencies may find the book particularly appealing as they seek to engage and strengthen better the organizations they support financially or otherwise. Students and teachers of organizational and community development and African studies will gain from the new use of indigenous cultures as a tool for development introduced in the book,

Lastly, the book will make good leisure and inspirational reading for anyone interested in indigenous wisdom and how it can be creatively applied to improve organizational performance in particular and modern life in general. It is hoped that the book will simplify and add humour to organizational language which is often covered in jargon and myth, especially for people who are not organizational specialists. Also that it will demystify organizational language while at the same time enhancing its power, and will make a contribution to cross-cultural dialogue which is a great need among organizations and societies today.

How to Use This Book

When I visited Washington to launch the first book, *Understanding Organisational Sustainability through African Proverbs*, a lot of people – especially Professor Coraile Bryant, then of Columbia State University – encouraged me to write a book on how people in general, including individuals, families, communities and countries, can use the wisdom in proverbs in modern life. They reasoned that the wisdom contained in the proverbs is more about people and applying it only to organizations may be limiting. Being an Organization Development Practitioner, I think I am still biased towards organizations, but I believe the principles and lessons discussed in the book can be extended to people in general as well. Instead of interpreting the title *Understanding Organizational Leadership through Ubuntu* as meaning or referring only to organizations, it may be more meaningful to understand it as meaning how individuals, families, organizations, communities etc. may organize themselves more effectively and humanely using the wisdom contained in the proverbs.

Readers interested in gaining an understanding of what organizations are and how they function and develop over time will find it necessary to go through the whole book. While each chapter is self-contained, organizations are complex systems and isolating topics may obscure this complexity. Those more interested in how proverbs can be used to understand organizations may find it useful to read the whole book or simply the chapters of greatest interest.

Those interested in improving organizational performance may treat the book as a resource and a guide to interventions. The material in the book may form good background reading to stimulate reflection both for the organizational capacity building service providers or practitioners and for the people in the organization going through the capacity building services process.

Specific organizational assessment tools are found at the end of each chapter and at the back of the book, and can be used or modified according the specific organizational situation. Since this book is a third in the series – *Understanding Organizational Sustainability through African Proverbs* and *Making Strategic Plans Work: Insights from African Indigenous Wisdom* being the first and second respectively – those who have not read the first two books may find it useful to obtain copies for a fuller understanding.

Some Lessons on Using African Proverbs from Practice

We have used African proverbs in Organization Assessment processes, strategic planning, team building, leadership development, board development and self-development interventions. We have also used African proverbs in working with a range of organizations including community based organizations (CBOs), professional NGOs or non-profit organizations, churches and government departments. From this experience we have learned a number of lessons.

In the proverbs based self-assessment tools (especially at the end of the book), the proverbs act as a 'communication aid or amplifier'. The participants discuss their understanding of the proverbs. They then apply this understanding when answering a question and determining the assessment rate and its explanation. We have also learned that it is often necessary to use an external facilitator to moderate the discussions and the self-assessment process.

It is necessary to use the most fitting proverb for the intervention or situation at hand. Using 'loose' proverbs without a clear link to the intervention or the situation may have the effect of confusing the people and disrupting the process. The practitioner must always ask himself or herself the question, what is the most effective proverb that I can use in this situation? In a roles and responsibilities clarification intervention, for example, proverbs like *If the sun says it is more powerful than the moon, then let it come and shine at night* and *The cat in his house has the teeth of a lion* may be very appropriate. In communicating the importance of learning from practice, a proverb like *A person is taller than any mountain they have climbed* would be appropriate.

In training workshops it is important to use only a few proverbs to maximize their impact. Too many proverbs may lead to loss of interest in the proverbs. This also applies to carrying out assessments using the proverbs based tools. In a three-day team-building workshop, for example, we use about three proverbs in one session at the beginning of the workshop to bring to the surface issues and insights for discussion. In the proverbs based assessment tool this may mean that not all categories may need the proverbs – only those for which proverbs will add significant value. In other words proverbs are more useful where a direct question may not bring out all the insights because people do not completely understand the question or the issue.

It is important to use reflective questions in order to bring out the insights from the proverbs. Since proverbs may mean different things to different people at different times and in different contexts, the questions must be properly phrased and focused to enable them to solicit only those insights related to the issue at hand. In a self-development session, for example, we use a question like: What insights on self-development can we learn from the proverb *A changed place cannot transform an individual but a transformed individual can change a place*? When we used this question and proverb with a rural CBO a chief explained his total agreement with the proverb by telling the group a story of an individual in his village who migrated to a neighbouring country, hoping to be 'transformed' by its better economy, and somebody else who came from that country to reside in his village. The person who came to reside in his village was a very productive individual and within a short time he became very wealthy. The person who migrated to the other country came back after a few years frustrated and poorer as the 'transformed nation' failed to transform him.

Proverbs can also be used as reflective case studies. To do this more effectively it is important to know and use the story upon which the proverbs are based. Using a story is especially useful on complicated issues, which are difficult to communicate. For example, it is extremely difficult to teach and communicate organizational identity issues, but using 'proverbs case studies' easily transcends such a barrier. In 'identity interventions', for example, we have used the story behind the proverb *An eaglet that does not know that it is an eagle may live like a chicken*. The story goes like this:

A farmer picked an egg from an eagle's nest. He placed it among the eggs a chicken was sitting on. When the eggs hatched, among the chicks was an eaglet from the eagle's egg. The eaglet and chicks moved and grew together. Because of its socialization, the eaglet took the personality of a chick and was growing into a chicken until one day when an eagle was flying over the chicken and the chicks and noticed the eaglet.

The eagle descended and hovered over the chicken and the chicks screaming apparently trying to call the eaglet. The chicken and the chicks became restless and afraid and were running for cover. The eaglet too became restless and afraid and was running for cover. In the process however the eaglet looked up and was immediately struck by its resemblance with the eagle. For the first time the eaglet saw that it was different from the chicken and the chicks. Instead of producing more fear, the screams of the eagle started to produce a magnetic attraction for the eaglet. The eaglet felt like getting close to the eagle. That moment the eaglet knew that it did not belong to the chickens anymore. The eaglet had never flown before. It tried to jump and the moment it did it flew away with mother eagle.

Discussion questions:

• What does the story of the eaglet teach us as an organization?

• How similar or different are we to the eaglet?

• What are we going to do in order to improve?

Finally, proverbs must be used naturally and flexibly, not mechanically. If used mechanically, the proverbs may actually become a hindrance to the process. The power of proverbs when used properly is their 'invisibility' as they serve to facilitate the process rather than draw attention to themselves. This means that proverbs must be used only when their use will add value to the process. Development practitioners must not get too excited with the use of proverbs to the extent of 'using crutches when they can walk on their own feet'.

The Organization of the Book

This book is divided into seven chapters. The first chapter introduces the African concept of personhood or the essence of being human called *ubuntu,* based on the proverb *The river that forgets its source will soon dry up.*

The second chapter discusses organizational and leadership lessons that organizations can learn from the *ubuntu* principle of taking responsibility through collective ownership of organizational challenges and opportunities. It is based on the proverb *Judge each day not by its harvest but by the seeds you sow into it.*

The third chapter discusses the primacy of people and relationships in organizations. It is based on the proverb *It is better to be surrounded by people than to be surrounded by things.*

The fourth chapter discusses participatory leadership and decision making in organizations. It is based on the proverb *If you want to go fast travel alone, if you want to go far travel with others.*

The fifth chapter addresses the principle of loyalty by discussing cultivation of professional and management excellence. It is based on the proverb *A person is taller than any mountain they have climbed.*

Chapter six discusses how organizations can manage their organizational conflicts more effectively. It is based on the proverb *There is not a river that flows without sounds.*

The seventh and last chapter discusses how organizations can improve their knowledge management efforts. It is based on the proverb *It is not money that builds a house but wisdom.*

Chapter 1

ORGANIZATIONAL LESSONS FROM *UBUNTU* CULTURES

The river that forgets its source will soon dry up

This chapter introduces the African concept of personhood commonly known as *ubuntu*. *Ubuntu* is a cultural worldview of what it means to be human, or simply the essence of being human (Malunga, 2006: 3). The English literal translation for *ubuntu* would be, 'I am because you are and you are because I am' (Mapadimeng, 2007: 258).

Three components make up an organization. These are its *being*, *doing* and *relating* (with its different stakeholders). The *being* represents the collective personhood of the people in the organization and their capacity. The collective personhood of the people in the organization is the source for achieving true organizational effectiveness. It is what makes synergistic relationships within and without the organization possible. *Ubuntu* therefore is the foundation upon which organizations can build a strong and sustainable foundation.

The results the organization produces are derived directly from its *doing* but indirectly from its *being* and *relating*. Hence most organizations concentrate most of their efforts on their *doing* or their project activities. But to be truly effective the organizations must become more conscious of the need to base their *doing* and *relating* on their *being*. Organizations need to consciously base their *doing* and *relating* on their being because it is the *being* that represents the true capacity of the organization. Organizations cannot give in their *doing* and *relating* what they do not have in their *being*. The proverb *The river that forgets its source will soon dry up* teaches that organizations that concentrate only on their *doing* and *relating* while forgetting their *being* will soon see their results drying up. This book focuses on how organizations can balance their being, doing and relating with special emphasis on the *being* or *ubuntu* which is often not given the attention it deserves.

The proverb *It is better to be surrounded by people than to be surrounded by things* illustrates the essence of *ubuntu*. *Ubuntu* is built on five interrelated people-centred principles: sharing and collective ownership of opportunities, responsibilities and challenges, the importance of people and relationships over things, participatory leadership and decision making, loyalty, and reconciliation as a goal of conflict management.

The positive elements of these principles will be discussed in turn and then applied to organizational development. It is important to mention at this point that there are some negative elements of *ubuntu* as well. Some of these negative elements arise from the fact that *ubuntu* principles were mainly practiced at village or community level in a very stable and predictable environment. Part of the challenge that *ubuntu* is facing today is that it has generally failed to change with time and transcend this stable and predictable context. This has resulted in certain 'shadows' being cast over the current practice of *ubuntu* values, such as:

- Loyalty to kinship developing into tribalism;

- The belief in kings and chiefs ruling for life, leading to modern elected leaders not respecting term limits in office;

- Fear of unpredictable futures, motivating leaders to try to accumulate as much wealth as possible, or succumb to corruption while in office;

- Values attached to relationships at the expense of personal progress, often leading to wasteful expenditure on, for example, births, weddings, initiation ceremonies and burials;

- The value of respect for elders may lead to blind loyalty to old ideas that may have stopped working; and

- The desire for 'continuity or survival of the village or clan' can undermine the need for radical change in response to rapidly changing environments.

To compound these problems, the trend towards globalization implicitly gives prominence to Northern values and can give the sense that non-Northern indigenous values and practices are somehow inferior. The low self-esteem that results from this has caused people in Africa and other developing regions to abandon their own values and embrace those from America and Europe. As a result cultural interchange of values from these different regions has suffered. Through the proverbs, this book aims to demonstrate that cultures like *ubuntu* have something of value to offer to life in Western societies in general and organizational improvement efforts in particular, just as these cultures are also able to benefit a lot from the Western cultures. At the end of the day what is important is to get the best of both cultures, to create a better and synergistic culture for the benefit of humanity and organizations.

Unfortunately, in the past and even today, the negative aspects of *ubuntu* have been overemphasized, with the effect of 'throwing away the baby together with the bath water', that is, throwing the good out with the bad. To redress this imbalance, in the following sections I have chosen to explore the positive aspects of the five principles of *ubuntu* and how they were applied in the past.

Sharing and Collective Ownership of Opportunities, Responsibilities and Challenges

A rooster may belong to one household but when it crows it crows for the whole village

Most indigenous African societies believed in taking collective responsibility. Children were seen as children of the community rather than belonging to their parents only. Discipline could be meted out by any adult member of the community. Children were taught to respect all adults the same way they respected their parents. Clan households collectively met responsibilities such as school fees and other expenses for the children.

When a visitor came to the community, they were a visitor to the whole community and not only for the household they were visiting. Members of the community would take responsibility for the visitor. They would be expected to make contributions for the visitor's upkeep or take it in turns to feed them. When a member of the community got sick, the whole community was affected. The members of the community would be expected to help in things like taking care of the children of the sick person or help them with gardening work. When a person died, the funeral was a community funeral.

Cooperation in work and life were encouraged, with real progress believed to be that which could benefit all. Those in privileged positions took it as their responsibility to help the less privileged to rise to positions of privilege as well, living by the saying that *A lit candle loses nothing by lighting another candle.* They were therefore not expected to be jealous of others rising to positions of privilege as well.

While collaboration was encouraged, each person was expected to contribute towards the wellbeing of the clan, according to his or her age, knowledge, skills and experience. No one was expected to be a parasite. They believed that *A person who is being carried does not realize how far the town is.* Only the very young, the old and the sick were exempted. They believed that problems were better solved by working together on the assumption that *Ants united can carry a dead elephant to their cave.*

The Importance of People and Relationships over Things

Kinship is like bone, it does not decay

In indigenous African communities relationships were given very high priority. Uncles were ranked the same as fathers. Aunts were mothers. Cousins were brothers and sisters. All adults were treated as one's parents.

When one married someone from another clan, one did not marry just the individual but the whole clan. When this happened, every member of the two clans became a relative. This also implied mutual responsibilities as in weddings, funerals, births, problems and any other celebrations. This is a meaning of an extended family.

Relationships were characterized by respect, especially by the young to the old. Children were taught that *What old men and women see while seated, they could not see even when standing on their toes.* They were taught that children who respected their parents would learn many things without their parents having to teach them. The closeness of family or clan was the beginning of African education. Family relationships were also informed by shared responsibilities, such that when a parent died, children would be automatically adopted by the family members and treated as one's own children.

The cohort that went through initiation ceremonies together became brothers or sisters for life – as strong a bond as a blood relationship. A school today rarely produces such an effect on classmates.

Participatory Decision Making and Leadership

Taking action based on one person's view is provoking wasps in a nest

At first glance, indigenous African leadership appears automatic and autocratic, but although some were born in the royal lineage, the approval of the people was critical for the legitimacy of newly elected leaders, as illustrated in the case below:

Stoning ceremonies

The Bafut kingdom of Cameroon installed their kings only after a candidate had been presented to the people for a 'stoning ceremony'. In the case of approval of a new leader the stones consisted of tiny harmless pebbles, but if the candidate was not desired the stones were large injurious rocks hurled to maim, chase off or even kill the proposed incumbent. It reminded the new ruler what would happen to him or her if their rule would become illegitimate. If the leader survived the coronation, dethronement was unlikely because systems were put in place to provide checks and balances to the king so that he/she did not defy accountability to the people.

Ritual acts and elements such as ceremonial objects with an established protocol of usage (e.g. a sceptre, crowns, utensils, stools and flywhisks) could not be used at the king's whim. These objects were invested with divine or ancestral power to inhibit their abuse. If the transfer of power from one leader to the other did not follow agreed procedures, the usurper of the throne would be disapproved by the gods, which would be evidenced by misfortunes arising from his or her attempted use of the sacred objects. These misfortunes would be in the form of sterility, madness or even death, and could extend to the people who colluded to instal the leader fraudulently. The misfortunes also applied to any rightful leader who turned against his or her own people

(Williams, 2002:61).

The accountability of leaders was reinforced because there were many possible candidates for leadership, so that strict criteria were applied to determine who would emerge as a leader. This decision was often subject to the approval of the people. Responsibility was a major determining factor because they believed that *No matter how blunt, a machete should never be held by a mad person.*

As Professor Michongwe explains (2005, personal communication), to emerge as a leader candidates had to show competence in: understanding people and human nature, understanding human relationships, conflicts and how to manage them, diplomacy and relationships with other kingdoms; the art of war; strategic thinking; and kingdom secrets and how to guard them.

Nelson Mandela (1994: 20) describes the profound influence that the democratic decision-making processes of the Tembu people (of which his grandfather was chief) had on him:

> Everyone who wanted to speak could do so. It was democracy in its purest sense. There may have been a hierarchy of importance amongst the speakers, but everyone was heard...Only at the end of the meeting as the sun was setting would the regent speak. His purpose was to sum up what had been said and form some consensus among the diverse options. But no conclusion was forced on those who disagreed.

While the king was the most visible leader and the indigenous custodian of power, auxiliary authorities – often people of highly respected religious or elder status – continually advised the king in roles that promoted democracy in the kingdom. Tangwa (1998:2) observed that while the king generally appeared very powerful from outside, he or she was nevertheless subject to very strict control, not only by means of taboos, but also from institutions and personalities whose main occupation was the protection and safeguarding of the people, the ancestors, the land and the unborn. Indigenous leadership, therefore, did not comprise solely the authority of the ruler, but was influenced by queen mothers, godfathers, councils, secret societies, mystics, rituals, ceremonies, rules and citizens. The king's decisions were continually subject to review by others (Mologtlegi, 2004:3).

A council of elders often played a key governance role in the kingdom, in a number of ways:

Custodianship of the kingdom. The elders were concerned with the welfare of the land, the living, the ancestors and the unborn. Individual chiefs or kings could come and go but the council was a permanent structure.

Advising the king. The king would use the council as a sounding board for his or her ideas and critical issues facing the kingdom. For example, on the occasion of identifying his or her successor, the chief would propose the name to the council which would discuss the issue and give its feedback.

Managing conflicts and disputes on behalf of the king in courts. The king only listened while the council dealt with cases. After a case was concluded, the council would meet the king or queen to give them its view. The king or queen would examine it against what he or she had heard. They then would come up with a joint stand and the king would announce the judgment.

Managing the transition from one king to the next. The council had to approve an identified candidate and mentor and coach them. If the king suddenly died, the council managed the transition to the next king by installing an interim ruler while initiating a process to identify a permanent ruler.

Installing or dethroning kings. The council had the power with the mandate of the people to dethrone a king or a queen whom it felt 'had gone astray' or was leading the kingdom astray. They would ask the king to resign, or they would ask him or her to voluntarily 'drink poison' to make way for a new king. This was a rare occurrence however, as the selection process and mechanisms put in place made the probability of a situation coming to this minimal.

Proposing new laws and changing laws that had become obsolete. Officially, the king was accountable to the gods through the council. The king could only overrule the proposals of the council if he sensed the council was in error. When this happened, the king had to give adequate explanation for his decision to convince the council, and this had to be accepted by the wider population.

Loyalty

The river that forgets its source will soon dry up

In all decisions the kingdom came before any personal interest. The reign of a particular king, however loved or hated, was never more important than the endurance of the kingdom itself. In some kingdoms, when the ruler was perceived to be a political liability, or if their continued reign was considered dangerous to the survival of the kingdom, he or she would be quietly executed or even asked to 'voluntarily' drink poison.

All the people had an understanding of the need for a common bond of security; they would not allow anything to endanger the security of the clan. People within the clan could disagree and quarrel, but people outside the clan were not allowed to take advantage through collusion with disgruntled members.

There was great emphasis on pride in one's clan. Each child was taught their origins, their family history, and they were encouraged to know and visit all members of the extended family, even those that were staying far away. People were continually reminded to respect their origins and identity by sending remittances and not abandoning their cultural values and practices, irrespective of where they were.

Reconciliation as a Goal of Conflict Management and Resolution

Those who live in peace work for it

Principles of conflict management emphasized the values of trust, fairness and reconciliation. This was closely linked with the importance of relationships. Conflict mediation and maintenance of relationships was a critical role of the king and the council.

The people were duty bound to attend court hearings and to ensure laws were upheld. As a result of this collective responsibility, everyone had a right to question in an open court. The concept of openness was an important value, implicit in which was the belief that no one should be punished for anything correctly said in an open forum (Jackson, 2002: 8).

Conflict was managed systematically through a hierarchy of levels. Smaller conflicts were resolved at family or household levels and proceeded to higher levels through appeal if some parties were not satisfied with the outcome. At higher levels, different levels of representatives of the king were responsible. The gravity or seriousness of the conflict determined the level at which it would be dealt with. Only very big cases would therefore reach the king's or the queen's court. The goal of all conflict mediation was reconciliation and relationship building. The notion of *ubuntu* emphasized the importance of peace making through principles of reciprocity, inclusivity and a sense of shared destiny between people. It provided a value system for giving and receiving forgiveness (Murithi, 2006: 6).

Indigenous African Leadership – Building on the Positives

The previous sections highlighted the key elements of many African cultures taking a more positive view of indigenous organization and leadership. In the following sections, building on the proverbs *The river that forgets its source will soon dry up* and *It is better to be surrounded by people than by things,* I will explore how the following principles of *ubuntu* may be applied to organizational development: collective responsibility for the organization, importance of relationships, participatory leadership, loyalty and reconciliation

The following sections will give an overview of the lessons that organizations can learn from the above principles. This discussion will be developed as each of the principles will form the basis of the subsequent chapters.

Taking Collective Responsibility for the Organization

Collective responsibility is key to organizational success. In many organizations, both leaders and followers place blame on each other, thereby abdicating responsibility. Blaming others for organizational challenges can dissipate the organization's energy and diminish its ability to address the challenges.

Collective responsibility also applies to the fair distribution of benefits and efforts. When some people are perceived as unjustifiably benefiting more than others from the organization's collective efforts, this will lead to resentment and strained relationships, adversely affecting team spirit and organizational performance. In addition, people must feel that others are pulling their weight in the organization. When people feel that they are 'selling more than they are buying', they may reduce their effort or opt out. This can kill the hard working and innovative spirit in the organization.

Importance of Relationships

The *ubuntu* emphasis on relationships may usefully be applied to leadership. Organizations can be viewed as extended families in which relationships are close enough to go beyond the professional level. In formal organizations, in contrast to indigenous communities, there is a tendency to not cross this boundary or interfere with people's personal lives outside the office – even though what is done outside the office may affect other staff and eventually the organization as well.

Like in extended families, it may be more appropriate to create an organizational environment where people feel close but also able to 'interfere' in other people's lives if they feel that would benefit the person and the organization.

Participatory Leadership

As with community leadership, appointments to positions of organizational leadership need to be conducted with complete

9

transparency and accountability. The process of selection must leave stakeholders satisfied with its fairness.

A symbolic 'stoning' ceremony for new leaders might be an important ritual to connect a new leader with the people in the organization. Such a ceremony could involve letting the people 'shoot' the leader with burning questions concerning issues facing the organization and how his or her leadership will make a difference.

Leadership development needs to emphasize the importance of involving people in addressing the challenges the organization is facing through meaningful participation. When people participate meaningfully, they will also own and commit to the identified solutions. In addition, the sense of belonging to the organization is enhanced.

Individual leaders should not be allowed to become too powerful. The important role of the councils, elders and healers in providing a check and balance on this power needs to be developed within the governance and internal systems of the organization. This is done primarily through ensuring that the organization has an effective and functional board, and that it has effective policies, systems and procedures that are being adhered to.

Loyalty

The *ubuntu* concept of loyalty means that organizational interests must always precede personal interests. Many leaders in organizations sacrifice long-term organizational interests for short-term self-interest. Leadership must be taken as an opportunity to serve rather than as a means to accumulate wealth and power.

No person should be more important than the organization, no matter how much that person is loved or hated. When a leader's continued existence in the organization becomes a danger to the organization's survival or wellbeing, they may need to be fired or asked to 'voluntarily drink poison' by resigning.

Organizations should also inculcate in their staff a culture of pride in their organization. In many organizations staff feel that there are better organizations out there and therefore do not make much commitment to their own. Managing the culture and performance of the organization helps leaders develop pride among staff. True commitment to an organization is based on people deeply and consciously connecting their values to those of the organization, so it is important to identify these personal values and link them to those of the organizational culture. Initiatives like mentoring, coaching, succession planning, and nurturing young and second tier leaders should emphasize the clarification and cultivation of values. One way of doing this is through adopting rituals from the people's cultural context. Rituals symbolizing success, growth and losses connect people to each other and their cultural values.

Reconciliation

The organizational mechanisms for conflict resolution must ensure fairness, trust, reconciliation and relationship building as the goal. People should have the right to appeal to higher levels if they are not satisfied with the outcome of the conflict mediation process.

The aim of conflict resolution must be to help people involved reach an agreement by consensus rather than forcing them to 'shake hands' before they feel that the issue has been resolved or justice has been administered. Giving and receiving forgiveness must provide the foundation for relationship building.

In a conflict situation involving a subordinate and a superior, great wisdom and discretion should be exercised to balance fairness, maintaining of respect, and avoidance of loss of face in the case of the senior party being in the wrong.

In the case of simple conflicts, leaders should delegate conflict management, encourage people to resolve these conflicts at a low a level as possible. This gives the people in higher positions more space and time to get involved in bigger and more strategic issues.

Implications for Organizational Development

A number of lessons are emerging from an understanding of the concept of *ubuntu* as discussed above. Among these are:

Emphasis, articulation and inculcation of values. Organizational and leadership development programmes must aim to transform individuals by touching people in the affective or values domain. Instead of a focus on what people should be able to *do* after the programmes, there should be more emphasis on what the people should *be* after the programmes. Programmes need to encourage participants to live up to their values. Organizational and leadership development must be about strengthening the values that guide behaviour through mentorship, coaching, placements and self-development programmes for example.

Use of proverbs, rituals and ceremonies as part of the organizational and leadership development process. An example of a ritual would be a symbolic 'stoning ceremony' for new leaders. As a ritual, this would connect the new leader with people in the organization. Such a ceremony could involve letting people tell the leader their expectations and fears.

Applying individual leadership development to the benefit of the organization. People must be empowered to take on training lessons beyond the classroom. Leadership development programmes should emphasize the principle that leadership is responsibility and service to the organization and the people the organization serves.

Viewing organizational and leadership development as long-term, if not life-long processes. The leadership needs and demands of the organization and the sectors are constantly changing, so long-term and life-long leadership development processes are necessary to adapt and to implement change effectively.

Planning leadership succession in advance. Organizations must plan for succession in good time, and have a clear and effective system for identifying their successors. The successors must undergo well thought through programmes that will prepare them to take charge of the organization when their times comes.

Involvement of the board in succession and organizational and leadership development planning. The board must ensure that appointments to leadership positions are conducted with complete transparency and accountability. The process followed to select new leaders must leave the people in the organization satisfied. Organizations must have succession plans well in advance to ensure smooth transitions from one leader to the next.

While the above suggestions may not be radically different from what any management guru would recommend, the value of the recommendations and their practice is the validation of the *ubuntu* model and the connection and ownership this model makes possible in connecting the people in the organization to their values and identity – to what is their own. This is the essence of people-centred leadership and organizational development.

Investing time, money and energy in its people and their development is the way an organization and its leadership can demonstrate commitment to being people-centred and show that the organization is interested in the people as people, not merely as things or resources for the achievement of its goals. This is the way an organization can demonstrate that it is indeed *better to be surrounded by people than to be surrounded by things*. This is the way of developing *ubuntu* or collective, responsible, humane, participatory, loyal, and reconciliatory leadership in the organization.

Conclusion

Based on the proverb *The river that forgets its source will soon dry up*, this chapter has argued that to be effective organizations need to build their doing or projects on a strong foundation of *being* and *relationships*. The being of the organization, it has been demonstrated, is based on the core defining values of *ubuntu* which are respect, group solidarity, conformity, compassion, human dignity and collective unity and responsibility, sharing, universal brotherhood, communalism, interdependence and hospitality (Mapadimeng, 2007: 25). These values represent the essence of personhood or humanness. Using proverbs, the next chapters will discuss in detail how the five principles of *ubuntu* can help improve organizational effectiveness, especially in building a strong *being* and *relating* foundation for the organizations. The principles, once again, are: sharing and collective ownership of opportunities, responsibilities and challenges; the importance of people and relationships over things; participatory decision making; leadership loyalty; and reconciliation as a goal of conflict management

Reflection Proverbs

What can we learn about organizations from these proverbs?

The river that forgets its source will soon dry up

A rooster may belong to one household but when it crows, it crows for the whole village

What old men and women see while sitting, the young may not see even standing on their toes

Taking action based on one person's view is provoking wasps in a nest

No matter how blunt, a machete should never be held by a mad person

How can we use those lessons to improve the effectiveness of our organization?

Organization Improvement Tool

Rate each of the elements below on a scale of 0 – 5. 0 = non-existent, 5 – excellent. Give an explanation for your rating.

Principles	Rate 0 - 5	Explanation
• Sharing and collective ownership of opportunities, responsibilities and challenges		
• The importance of people and relationships over things		
• Participatory decision making and leadership		
• Loyalty and commitment to the organization by staff		
• Effectiveness of conflict management and resolution practices		

From the above rating what are the strengths and limitations of our organization? What can we do to build on the strengths and address the limitations?

Chapter 2

RESPONSIBILITY BASED DEVELOPMENT

Judge each day not by its harvest but by the seeds you sow into it

Introduction

Collective ownership as a principle is meant to add value and create synergy to individual and group efforts. Collective ownership, if not well understood, may however produce the shadow of dependence or 'sponging'. In Africa especially sponging is a big challenge constraining economic development. When one member of a family is making progress and is financially better off the whole clan wants to benefit. The person is put under obligation to take care of the whole clan. At the end of the month the whole clan may come with all sorts of bills to the individual. By spreading himself or herself too thinly the person cannot make any significant personal progress. He or she is held back. If anyone refuses to help, they are branded selfish and unpatriotic. Helping has its place, but it should not be at the expense of sustainable personal progress. One must take care of oneself before one can take care of others. Forgetting this makes all help non-developmental. There is such a thing as personal responsibility where every person must take care of themselves and not depend on others.

It is important to always follow one's own agenda even if one may be branded ruthless or inhuman. It is important to strike a balance and as much as possible avoid being sidetracked by others' demands. Personal effort and achievement must be rewarded and it is wrong to think that just because we are related those who worked hard to achieve and those who did not must have the same economic status. It is personal and collective effort and achievement that have driven economic development all over the world, and personal effort and achievement cannot be substituted.

A related problem is the culture of not paying back money and other things borrowed from friends. Many Africans are very kind and want to help each other. Sometimes people even use their capital to lend to friends in need, but often borrowed money will not be returned. There is this feeling that if he could lend me this money then he must have more. This thinking and practice have led to the demise of many promising businesses. Books, tapes, CDs, DVDs once borrowed usually don't come back. Personally, after many disappointments I have come up with a personal policy that I will not lend anyone any money, except for two friends who have never disappointed me, and I will follow this policy very religiously. The fastest way to kill businesses and relationships is through borrowing and lending without paying back.

The problem of sponging is not entirely or exclusively an African problem. It happens in other societies as well, including America. I was watching an Oprah Winfrey show the other day where this subject was being discussed. Many people including some celebrities were explaining how their lives were made difficult or even ruined because of sponging from irresponsible relatives. One person said he used to get bills for expensive items like cars, refrigerators, designer clothes at the end of the month from shop owners who told him his relatives got the items on the basis that he would pay; as he was the famous person that he was, the dealers did not see any problem with this.

In discussing the concept of collective ownership, therefore, I deliberately concentrate on taking responsibility as my main subject of discussion. I present some reflective thoughts from my own practice on the primacy of taking responsibility as a key foundation for organizational and practice effectiveness. A key concept I would like to introduce is 'surfacing and confronting contradictions'. Taking responsibility for organizational and practice effectiveness often means the ability to 'surface and confront our contradictions' as individuals, organizations, communities and even countries.

Collective ownership only becomes useful when everyone takes responsibility to make their best contribution. This creates 'synergy'. When people abdicate responsibility and start pointing fingers at each other the organizational energy to address challenges and take advantage of opportunities is dissipated.

Sowing and Harvesting

Judge each day not by its harvest but by the seeds you sow into it

Each seed produces its own kind. The harvest is a reflection of the seeds that were sown. If we are happy with the harvest, we need to sow more seeds of the same. If we are not happy with the harvest, we need to change the seeds we sow. Linking harvest and seed is a rare skill in personal, family, organizational or even national life. People get caught up in celebrating the harvest of success, forgetting what produced that harvest in the first place. They get caught up complaining about the harvest of failure, forgetting or not linking with what produced the harvest of failure in the first place.

A key to developing oneself, one's organization or one's community is to take a reflective stance. Such a practice enables one to consciously link the results one is observing to their causes or seeds. It enables one to *Judge each day not by its harvest but by the seeds you sow into it.* This practice enables corrective action in the case of a wrong harvest. It also enables improvement in the case of a desired harvest. In short, it makes concentration for success possible – concentration of the resources of money, time and energy. Judging each day not by its harvest but by the seeds we sow into it forces us to focus on what happens inside us rather than what happens outside, because what happens outside is merely a reflection of what happens inside us. It forces us to focus on our *being* more than our *doing*. It helps us to confront and surface contradictions between what we truly want and what we are. It helps us to take responsibility for the results we are producing.

Common approaches used and promoted by NGOs, non-profit organizations and their donors like Participatory Rural Appraisal (PRA), Appreciative Inquiry (AI) or Millennium Development Goals (MDGs) processes focus on helping communities, organizations and nations plan their desired future. They emphasise external actions – the 'doing'. This is a necessary stage of a change process, but it is not sufficient. By merely making ambitious development plans, we either externalize or trivialize the problem – saying in effect that if we do 'a', 'b' and 'c' then 'd' will definitely result. We know from bitter experience that this is not the simplistic, deterministic way development or change occurs. Authentic change takes place at a deeper internal level – the 'being'. People's consciousness, commitment and sense of responsibility must be awakened for change to occur.

For development to take place, people must change behaviour, and this requires them to become aware of and then confront the contradictions in their past and current behaviour. Just as *When you point a finger of blame at another, the remaining four are pointing back at you,* individuals, communities, organizations and nations must avoid externalizing the problem as 'someone else's fault' or 'someone else's duty to assist' and begin to take responsibility for their contributions to the current context of problems. When asked what their development problems are people will usually produce long lists of problems, but they will rarely include themselves as a problem in the lists. But often the man in the mirror is the biggest culprit; as some people have said, *You are the only problem you will ever have and you are also the only solution.*

A 'responsibility-based approach' to development is essential if we are to release the will and energy to change. This book, written from the receiving end of a plethora of many development innovations and fashions developed in America and Europe, argues that development only occurs when people, communities, organizations and nations confront their contradictions and take responsibility for doing something about the problem themselves. It argues that development occurs when *people begin to judge each day not by its harvest but by the seed they sow into it.*

Realities of Change

A young man recently came to an HIV clinic in Zimbabwe where a friend of mine, Carol, works. When his voluntary test came out negative he was obviously relieved and delighted. So Carol asked him: 'What will you then do to remain negative?' He replied: 'I will be faithful to my wife at all times, even though she lives in the village while I stay in town. But if "nature comes" I will always use a condom.' He then asked for a packet of condoms. Carol congratulated him for his resolve, but instead of giving him one packet she gave him two packets of condoms. He was surprised and asked: 'What is the other packet for?' Carol replied: 'It is for your wife. Take it and give it to her to use when "nature comes" on her also.' The young man looked confused and asked my colleague to repeat what she had said. He went out of the clinic leaving both packets of condoms behind. A few days later he reappeared at the clinic beaming, this time together with his wife who was now staying with him in town. He said to Carol: 'We have come to thank you for what you said to me. It had never occurred to me that my wife has a "nature" too. After leaving your clinic I went home to the village and made arrangements for my wife to join me living in town.'

My wife told me a story of a friend whose husband was threatening to stop making public appearances with her unless she lost her weight considerably. She tried to lose her weight until she couldn't lose any more but the husband was still not impressed. When she realized that she could not lose any more weight, the wife began to think of ways to make her husband change his mind. She came up with a brilliant idea. She told her husband that she too would only make public appearances with her husband if the husband regained his lost hair on his head or if he reversed the balding process which was advancing at a very fast rate. This brought the husband's unrealistic demand to an end.

These stories illustrate, at an individual level, the development process of confronting your contradictions in order to change. This same process is repeated at a community, organizational, national and even international level. For example, some time ago we were working with a community water project in a rural area. The community members were not paying their minimal monthly financial contributions and this was jeopardizing the sustainability of the water supply. As we travelled round a number of villages we asked people: 'Why are you not paying for the water?' Some frequently answered: 'We are poor and do not have money.' Others said: 'The water should be free because the big development agency involved is very rich and can afford to meet all the costs with their "financial muscle".' Still others questioned: 'We are not sure that the money we give would even be used for maintaining the water supply. It might be eaten.'

We started by asking them: 'Where were you getting water before the "piped" water provided by the project?' They responded that there were other water sources, but these were unsanitary. We then asked: 'What were the consequences of using those sources?' They said they got sick from diarrhoea and dysentery and sometimes cholera. We asked them: 'So where did you go for treatment?' They said that because there were rarely any medicines in free government hospitals, they were forced to go to private hospitals and clinics, which were more expensive. Before we finished asking them these questions they were already seeing the contradictions arising out of their non-payment. They were paying at the private hospitals or clinics many times more than what was demanded for the water project. We went further to ask them: 'How would you feel if someone took over all your responsibility for your families and did everything for you? What would happen to your dignity? Would your self-respect be enhanced or diminished? What would your children and spouses think about you?' We also probed their fears about the financial mismanagement, asking them, 'Has there been a case of financial abuse that you think might reoccur?' They answered, 'No, nothing like that has ever happened.' So we said they should perhaps ask themselves instead, 'What if your money would not be abused?' This simple process of people realizing the inherent contradictions in their behaviour led them to take responsibility for solving the development problem, and the monthly contributions dramatically went up.

At national level we are often left frustrated by our leaders refusing to address the clear contradictions such as conspicuous consumption and corruption in government. Yet the profound example of Nelson Mandela emerging from 27 years' incarceration to preach forgiveness and unity prevented the widely predicted bloodbath to accompany the transition from apartheid. The Truth and Reconciliation Commission that he later set up to deal with the atrocities had no power to punish, only to listen and hear and grant amnesty. This difficult process was a very profound national example of confronting the excruciating contradiction of hearing the depths of inhumanity that people had descended to and being able to respond only with forgiveness, not revenge.

At an international level there seem to be precious few examples of us really confronting our contradictions to move forward, though the Jubilee 2000 debt campaign stands out as an exception. International trading relations, so clearly replete with such contradictions, remain largely impervious to fundamental change. For example, for aid to resume to Malawi, the country where I come from, the IMF recently required Malawi to implement sweeping changes to the government support to poor farmers through privatizing the agriculture marketing board and reducing fertilizer subsidies. When asked about the double standards of US subsidies for steel or EU subsidies for agriculture, the head of the IMF delegation mumbled: 'Yes, we disagree with those too, but there is nothing we can do about those.' Refusing to face such contradictions prevents authentic international development.

A Responsibility-Based Approach - The Process of Confronting Contradictions

If I had not been in prison I would not have been able to achieve the most difficult task in life, and that is changing yourself – Nelson Mandela

If you treat well the cat in your hands the one in the tree will come down of its own accord

The essence of a turning point in development or change processes is when people confront their contradictions and take responsibility for the solutions themselves. It is when people begin to *Judge each day not by its harvest but by the seeds they sow into it*. We cannot change the external situation before changing the internal situation. The internal situation is the only one we have some control over. Yet our tendency is to try to 'conquer outer space while ignoring inner space'.

Research among non-profit leaders (James 2003) into their change processes as leaders highlighted the importance of internal change being at the centre of external change. James found that leaders changed when they were confronted with information that considerably challenged their preferred ways of leading, they entered a crucible experience. Like all of us their instinctive reaction was denial and to externalise the blame. The respondents were able to move beyond blaming others and accepted responsibility for it. But even when they accepted responsibility for a problem, they had not arrived. They found themselves in an *"internal battle"*. This was not a pleasant place to be. It was a dark and confused place. Many of us prefer not to venture into our depths as we are frightened or ashamed of what we will find. If we dare enter our 'hearts of darkness', we have to be courageous to resist the temptation to quickly flee. Change occurred in the respondents when they realised that who they thought they were and who they actually were, were two different people. There was a realisation that what they believed about themselves and how they were behaving were not the same things. To a degree this challenged their very identity.

This process of confronting contradictions is an essential element in development and all change processes. As George Santayana said: 'Those who cannot remember the past are condemned to repeat it' (quoted by Tutu 1999). But it is often avoided because it is too painful to look inside, have our consciences awakened and accept the weight of responsibility for making change happen.

The Face of Change

A pioneer missionary noticed, among the Masai he had been teaching, an old man named Keriko in obvious pain. He was certain the old man was ill. But his Masai catechist, Paul, chuckled at his concern. He said: "Are you worried about old man Keriko? Don't worry he is all right. You see, for a Masai there is not much need to think in life. At most everything he learns, he learns by memory or by rote...he learns about food, clothes, houses, cattle, grasses and women by memory...even things about God and religion. When he needs an answer to a question, all he has to do is to reach into his memory and come up with the correct answer. He can reach adulthood without thinking at all. What you are asking Keriko to do is to take the first thought about Masai brotherhood and the second thought of the human race and the God of all tribes and put these two thoughts together to make a new thought. This is a very difficult work. What you are witnessing in Keriko is the pain on the face of a man who is thinking for the first time in his life."

Source: Smith (2001: 250-1)

The 'pain on the face of a person who is thinking' is someone confronting their contradictions. We rarely witness this pain in our development and change efforts. In fact we try to avoid it. Instead we see the increasingly tired and superficial smiles of people being promised that change will come – from the outside, from us, from the government. Development and change efforts fail when they do not challenge individuals, communities and organizations to make the link between their situations and their own decisions and actions (choices). It is only the pain of this link that catalyses developmental motion. The more pain people experience, the more they will be willing to confront themselves and bring creative change.

The Gaps in Current Development Approaches

We recently visited an African village which boasted 15 projects implemented by 10 different non-profit organizations. There were projects dealing with HIV/AIDS; Community School Development; Safe Motherhood; Breast Feeding; Food Security; Environmental Management; Gender; Human Rights; Child Rights; Water Supply; Income Generating Activities; Radio Listening Clubs; Civic Education; Orphan Care; and Aged People Support. The different non-profits used a plethora of different development approaches and tools including PRA, PLA, Training for Transformation, Appreciative Inquiry, PHAST, and Theatre for Development and 'the 9-point method'. Most non-profit bodies had their own committees and some individuals in the village belonged to as many as six different committees. The people in the village could have an average of three meetings per day with officers from the different organizations. Each of the organizations gave the people an allowance for attending a meeting – the breast feeding committee was the most coveted because its organization gave the highest allowances even though there was no problem about breast feeding in the village.

Ten years of incessant development activity had brought no significant change. Most of the development approaches used did not take the confronting of contradiction seriously enough. By missing out the painful essence of a change process, they also avoid mobilizing the necessary energy and passion for change. Looking at many of the popular approaches to development, such as PRA, Appreciative Inquiry, Rights Based Approaches and Sector Wide Approaches, we can see how in practice (though perhaps not in theory) this essential element of change is ignored.

PRA has undoubtedly revolutionized community development approaches by putting people, especially the vulnerable, at the centre of planning processes. Yet PRA in practice often misses out the contradiction stage. A PRA process rarely asks: what type of people must we be to realize our vision? What prevents us from realizing our vision? What must we change in ourselves in order to realize our vision?

PRA tends to be 'externally' rather than 'externally and internally' focused. The process often tends to emphasize that the 'oppressor' is out there in the environment. While this is usually true, a greater 'oppressor' is often in the people themselves. Until the people have come to see this fact, they will keep externalizing and not owning their challenges.

In organizational capacity building the appreciative inquiry (AI) approach has redressed the problem-oriented approach to change. It has demonstrated the need for a clear, inspiring and shared vision as the engine for development as well as for positive introspection as a means of self-discovery. AI has shown the importance of feeding an individual's or a group's strength and starving the weaknesses, and focusing on solutions rather than problems.

But like PRA, AI misses out the contradiction stage, failing to ask the difficult questions related to contradictions in past behaviour. An authentic development process demands that between 'what is' and 'what might be', people must explore their contradictions. But AI in practice tends to downplay the reasons why they are not in their 'what might be' yet. AI tends not to provoke sufficient crisis and pain, which are the antidote for inertia and prerequisites for developmental motion. Trying to help people move towards their vision without addressing contradictions is like applying the accelerator while at the same time as keeping your foot firmly on the brakes.

Rights-based Approaches (RBA) theory acknowledges that responsibilities are the other side of the coin, but the emphasis is still on my rights. A few years ago my then six-year-old daughter came back from school excited by a new poem she had learnt called 'my rights'. She recited perfectly:

> *Good education is my right*
> *Good clothes is my right*
> *Good food is my right*
> *Privacy is my right*
> *A name is my right*
> *Medical care is my right*

> *Unbiased information is my right*
> *Choosing my friends is my right*

I asked her if she had also leant another poem called 'my responsibilities'. She looked confused and said 'No Daddy'.

In a similar vein we were recently working with a women's rights non-profit organization, whose mission is to empower women to know, claim and practice their rights (on such issues as property grabbing by a man's relatives when the husband dies). In our work we observed in one family that both married sons had died, but property was only grabbed from one of the daughters-in-law. When we asked why, they said that one of the daughters-in-law had 'become one of them' through the way she had nurtured good relations with the extended family, so how could they take property from 'one of their own'?

In relationships one cannot do evil but to oneself and one cannot do good but to oneself.

When we mentioned this to our client non-profit organization they were not pleased. They felt that women had no responsibility for addressing the problem themselves and that by trying to show women contradictions in their behaviour that might exacerbate property grabbing, this would take them away from their mandate of 'purely teaching the women to know, claim and practice their rights'. They felt this was all that was necessary for development to occur.

Similarly on a national level, the Poverty Reduction Strategy Paper (PRSP) processes moves people towards agreed poverty reduction outcomes based on the analysis of causes of poverty and the strategy design. The need for the country to go through a contradiction process is rarely mentioned.

All these approaches to development at different levels have in common the notion that development external activity is the way of moving from the current situation to a desired situation.[1] This can be illustrated by the common development model below:

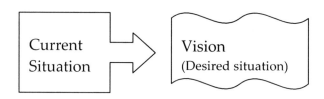

In reality development processes encounter a wall of contradiction as illustrated in a simplified linear way below:

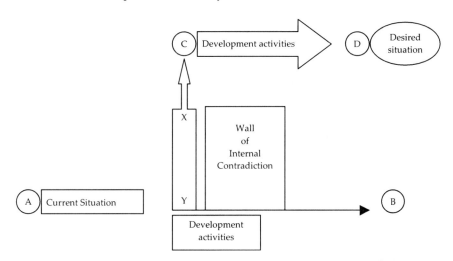

Development activities on AB cannot make people realize their vision (desired situation). Development activities can only help people to realize their vision if these are being implemented on CD. For people to work at CD level they must overcome the wall of internal contradictions by moving up the XY line. This is the conscious action of *judging each day not by its harvest but by the seed we sow into it.*

The more we begin to see the demands development makes on us, the more we will begin to understand that the 'being' must precede the 'doing'. Development efforts therefore must focus on both. If the 'being' does not change it can only reproduce the 'doing' of today and no more. It is incapable of doing differently. Any attempt to improve the doing without changing the being will only result in failure at worst and unsustainable improvements at best. People cannot get to a higher level without understanding how they were responsible for the lower level where they are today.

Implementing a Responsibility-Based Approach in Practice

We have shown that the missing element in most development processes is the contradiction stage – the failure to *Judge each day not by its harvest but by the seed we sow into it.* We have also shown that most development efforts concentrate on and emphasize how to help people get out of their undesired situations. They do not attach the same importance on why people are in their undesired situations. The

25

emphasis is on external factors and not the human (*responsibility*) factors creating and maintaining the status quo. Development is the awakening of consciousness – the consciousness of one's obligations and responsibilities. This is our main task in development.

But how exactly do we do this? How do we help people see the contradictions in their lives? How do we help them to *Judge each day not by its harvest but by the seeds they sow into it?* How do we help people to confront their shadows so that they can liberate themselves on their paths of development?

A responsibility based approach involves faith, relationship, heart-felt vision, confronting contradiction, and strategizing and implementing. A brief description of each follows.

Faith. Saying that the poor are responsible for their own development makes intellectual sense. But seeing the realities of people and their problems, such assent is an act of 'faith'. As development practitioners we need to honestly ask ourselves whether we really believe that the people we are working with can fundamentally change. If we have lost this faith and become cynical through disillusioning experiences, it is better to leave the development field. Sadly too many employees of the 'development industry' do not really believe that the people they are trying to help can change. They are reluctant to give responsibility to the people they work with because they consider it to be too risky for 'purposes of accountability'. But as Bentley advises: 'The risk involved in allowing the freedom of decision making is that (people) may be left floundering, unsure how to proceed, prone to making hasty decisions. The best way to offset this risk is not to prescribe rules and impose decisions, but to encourage reflection and critical discussion, and to make sure that appropriate guidance is available when the (people) seek it...this helps the people to develop their capacity to govern themselves.' (1998:47)

Relationship. A development practitioner must establish a relationship of mutual respect and trust with the people he or she is trying to help. Development occurs best within a relationship characterized by warmth, trust and mutual respect. The goal is for the development practitioner and the people he or she is trying to help to become comfortable with each other. This may mean staying in an area for some time

It is better to be surrounded by people than to be surrounded by things

creating rapport with the people before starting any 'visible' projects.

26

Attending weddings, funerals, traditional court cases, visiting people in their homes, attending communal events, visiting people in the gardens and learning the local language are some of the ways to achieve this. These activities not only help the practitioner to create relationships of trust with the people but also help him or her to understand the people better. Understanding the people's mindset is key to unlocking their potential.

Heart-felt vision. In the early 2000s many developing countries developed their 'Vision 2020' – an ideal picture of what a country should be by the year 2020. Today in most these countries almost no one remembers what that vision said and no one is talking about it. What has gone wrong?

We believe that a vision must engage people's emotions if it is to be motivating. During a nationwide consultation in 2002 on people's experiences, feelings and aspirations we were surprised to find how many people and communities could not articulate their desired futures. The general attitude was that things have always been bad. They are now getting worse, so how can we logically hope for a better future? My colleague related a story in one community of how when he was a child in a family of eight children they all used to go to visit their grandparents in their village. He said they could sometimes stay for three months at the grandparents' home and they did not need to bring anything from town because the grandparents were self-sufficient. He said that today, if he wants to go and see his parents in the rural home with his four children, he has to come with all the supplies with him from town, otherwise they will starve. The reaction to the story was telling; the young people in the group laughed and thought he was joking, because they had not seen a grandparent who could host ten visitors from town for three months without needing their support. The elder members agreed and but looked very concerned. They asked, 'What has gone wrong with us, where did we miss it?'

> *What the eyes have seen, the heart cannot forget*

Developing a genuine and authentic vision with people who have lost hope requires us to engage people's emotions. If a people is without hope, rational, intellectual planning is meaningless. Nothing will change, whatever plans are put in place. As a result we try and touch people's emotions in facilitating any development work. We ask questions like: 'What type of a country or what type of life do you want your children to live when they grow up?' We need to see our desired futures with our hearts.

Such a vision crafting process kindles a fire in the community. It creates motivation and enthusiasm. People start feeling pulled to their desired future. Their next natural questions are 'When shall we get there?' or 'How shall we arrive there?' We must avoid the temptation to jump into strategizing and leapfrog the crucial contradiction stage, where people are challenged to confront their shadows.

Confronting contradiction. An effective development process combines a vivid inspiring picture of where you want to go with a hard, convicting understanding of where you are now and why. It is this gap that is the source of pain and motivation for developmental motion. A development practitioner must find a way of intensifying the brilliance of both the vision and the current reality as a way of maintaining the pain and motivation.

The climax of the contradiction stage is when people see that the future is not arrived at accidentally but is created through our decisions and actions – our choices. People need to understand that just as the future is created through choices, the present was also created by the decisions and actions of yesterday. A development practitioner may need to challenge people to seriously reflect on how their choices yesterday have created the current undesired situation. People need to ask themselves: 'What have I been doing or not doing that has contributed to the current undesired situation?' Honest introspection can lead to healthy surfacing of contradictions and a clear understanding of what needs to be changed in ourselves. Now people are taking responsibility for change.

We need to ask developmental questions that reveal to people why they have not got the results they want. And show them that getting the results is largely within their 'circle of influence' – and therefore their responsibility. We are not asking ourselves the right questions and we might do well to learn from the example below.

When people have undergone a contradiction, they are more determined to own and be involved in the creation of their desired future. It is only then that such concepts as participation and involvement become meaningful. The next stage therefore is for the development practitioner to support the people and constantly keep them focused on the vision while further challenging them to recognize further contradictions on the way and deal with them.

Strategizing and implementing. The next challenge is how to maintain momentum and motivation and how to help people not to fall back to old ways. People need rewards and incentives to change. The development practitioner must help the people to recognize and celebrate their successes, no matter how small. He or she must help them to see how their taking responsibility is paying off. The development practitioner must also help them to understand that setbacks are normal and that they are part of the process.

In practical terms, it is important to create time for reflection and learning. The reflection and learning sessions must focus on achievements and failures of the initiatives and linking of these to taking responsibility and making choices. The learning sessions should show how the people's choices led to the achievements and failures. The more people see these links the more they will believe that they indeed create their own destinies.

The action point of such reflections is to encourage the people to take more responsibility to achieve more and address their challenges. The development practitioner must always maintain an attitude of support and challenge along the process. The results of each reflection and learning session must be documented and each subsequent session must be built on the previous ones. This helps to build increasing consciousness along the process. It helps the people to see how the journey is progressing. Monitoring and evaluation systems and management information systems and procedures therefore must include the 'consciousness raising' component. They must generate data that will be used to demonstrate how taking or abdicating responsibility will affect the progress of the project and therefore the attainment of, or the failure to attain, the vision.

Conclusions on Responsibility Based Development

If you really want to go to Mount Olympus make sure every step you make takes you nearer there – Socrates

We keep learning from bitter experience that we cannot change other people. Personal development is a personal responsibility. Organizational development is the organization's responsibility and similarly national development is a national responsibility. All development is self-development. No person can develop another and no country can develop another. They can only assist or hinder the development of the other. *The sympathizer cannot mourn more than the bereaved.* As development practitioners all we can do is create the conditions for people to become aware of their contradictions and encourage them to respond. This is not a very easy approach to sell to donors, clients or even our own egos. It means that we give up our vain attempts to command other people, communities and nations to develop and control them. This leaves us with the pain of having to stand by when people refuse to confront their contradictions and change. In his closing speech at the 2004 International HIV/AIDS conference in Thailand, Nelson Mandela said, 'We know what we should do, what is missing is the *will* to do it.' In other words we want a good harvest without sowing the right seed.

We cannot dictate other people's choices, however tempting that is. We cannot force people to confront their contradictions. But we can create the conditions and situations where this is more likely to happen. We need to design it into our change processes, rather than hope it happens by accident.

This chapter has shown that awakening the consciousness of individuals', families', communities', organizations' and nations' responsibility and obligation for own development through contradiction and self-confrontation processes is the way towards truly sustainable development. It is much more than simply planning, *The river that forgets its source will soon dry up.* monitoring and evaluating new activities. We need to focus on how people need to *'be'* to make the initiatives more effective, and sustainable. Ultimately people's *'doing'* cannot rise above their *'being'*. Similarly, the doing of the development worker or the change agent cannot rise above his or her being, as is emphasized by the saying *Who you are speaks so loud I can't hear what you are doing.*

Just as the slave trade came to an end when people confronted their shadows; colonization came to an end when people confronted their shadows; one-party states and life presidencies came to an end when people confronted their shadows; apartheid in South Africa came to an end when people confronted their shadows, so the global, continental, national, and societal challenges we are facing today will only be addressed when we have the courage to confront our contradictions. *Many people smear themselves with mud and then complain that they are dirty.* Unless people realize that they are dirty because they smeared themselves with mud, they will not change. People must be helped to realize that *If they climb a tree they must climb down the same tree.* This is the essence of contradiction and responsibility based development.

Conclusion on Collective Ownership of Organizational Responsibilities, Challenges and Opportunities

Organizational efforts aimed at encouraging collective ownership of organizational challenges, like consultation with staff, working groups, showing feedback to staff and demonstrating to staff that they have been listened to, often encounter problems, especially from those who have not 'bought in'. By using the *ubuntu* values of involving people at all stages and at all levels in the organization, encouraging openness and giving people good and clear feedback, they will be able to instill a sense of responsibility in the individuals and groups.

Real Play

Real play involves facilitating a discussion and reaching a consensus based on the gap between the vision and where the organization is today. Different people see the same situation differently. This is why it is important to discuss until they reach consensus. This exercise is especially suited for organizations undergoing serious challenges. After the consensus has been reached, it is important to let the people reflect individually and then in groups and finally in plenary on the following questions:

- Do you believe our situation can be described as a crisis? (people need to be in enough discomfort or pain to overcome developmental inertia)

- If so, what type of crisis is it? (pinpoint the main issues characterizing the crisis)?

- How have I personally contributed to the crisis?

- How have we as a community or organization or nation contributed to the crisis?

- What changes do I therefore need to make in myself?

- What changes do we need to make therefore in ourselves as a community or organization or nation?

It is important not to go through the process of answering the above questions superficially. Often people would like to rush and get through the questions as soon as possible, missing the essence of the questions in the process. Depending on the situation, going through this exercise must take at least a full day to at most a full week.

Taking responsibility means that people recognize that there are many things they cannot do anything about, but also that there are some things they can do something about, and then decide to concentrate on those things they can do something about. Taking responsibility therefore means concentrating on the individual's or organization's circle of influence.

Reflection Proverbs

What can we learn about taking personal and organizational responsibility from the following proverbs?

Judge each day not by its harvest but by the seeds you sow into it

If you treat well the cat in your hands, the one in the tree will come down of its own accord

The sympathizer cannot mourn more than the bereaved

Many people smear themselves with mud and then complain that they are dirty

If you climb up a tree you must climb down the same tree

How can we use the lessons to improve the sense of collective ownership and responsibility for our organization's success?

Note

[1] This is a description of how PRA, AI, and PRSPs are practiced in Malawi and many other places. In some cases good practitioners are able to assist people face their contradictions using these methods. But this is not a specific goal of these approaches.

Chapter 3

PEOPLE AND RELATIONSHIPS IN ORGANIZATIONS

It is better to be surrounded by people than to be surrounded by things

Introduction

In this chapter, I will discuss the concept of extended families and how it can be applied to organizations to make them more people-centred, especially as far as the staff and volunteers are concerned. The concept of people-centred development is common among organizations. Usually people-centredness is taken to be synonymous with being customer- or client-oriented. Organizations are now operating in a customer economy in which the customer is truly king (Hammer, 2003: 1). In the age of over-choice or an abundance of every product and services of almost everything, organizations simply have to work very hard at pleasing the customer or the customer will simply walk to the shop next door.

In trying to please the customer or client, however, it is possible that the organization forgets its own people who are serving the customer or the client. It is like the story of the little child who was asked to count the number of people in a room – he counted everyone and forgot himself – or the story of the child who cried that she had only nine fingers and not ten because she forgot to include the finger she was using in counting the other fingers. The point is, in trying to help others it is possible to forget oneself.

Ubuntu emphasizes that people and relationships, not only the ones being served but also the ones serving them, are important in achieving goals. Organizations can only be truly customer- or client-centred if in serving those customers and clients they are also centred on their primary customers and clients who are the staff. Happy staff and volunteers will mean happy customers and clients. Peter Drucker in Harvard Business Review (2006: 53) noted that in many organizations, managers or leaders no longer chant the old mantra, *People are our greatest asset.* Instead they claim that *people are our greatest liability.*

I am using extended families as a model for understanding and improving relationships in organizations and making them more people-centred. Handy (2006: 186) asserts that to describe organizations we need to use the language of communities and the language of individuals and to combine the needs of the individuals – and, I would add, their families – with the purpose of the large community to which they belong. He goes on to argue that we cannot divide life. Life is life whether in the family or at the office. The way we learn, the way we relate to the people we need or to those we have to live with, these can all provide lessons for the workplace.

Every model has its limitations and this one is no exception. In much of the West the concept of an extended family may invoke negative feelings as it may be associated with undue dependence, sponging, slowing down of individual progress and self-perpetuation of the family as a goal in itself without any specific contribution to society as families are not organizations. With this full understanding, this chapter intends to focus solely on the human values in families and extended families that can play a key maintenance role in organizations. For most people, organizations are our second if not only home. We spend most of our 'waking hours' in our organizations. Colleagues at work are the people we see most. I want to emphasize once again that I am using 'extended family' only in a metaphorical sense: that is, I am concentrating only on those attributes and values of family that would add value if adopted in organizations. I recognize the shadow that the downside of family can bring when taken wholesale to organizations and businesses, for example. I will use the metaphor of bees in a hive to emphasize the family values that organizations can adopt. Organizations can be viewed as extended families in which relationships are close enough to go beyond the professional level. In formal organizations, in contrast to indigenous communities, there is a tendency not to cross this boundary or interfere with people's personal lives outside the office – even though what is done outside the office may affect other staff and eventually the organization as well.

Like in extended families, it may be more appropriate to create an organizational environment where people feel close but also able to 'interfere' in other people's lives if they feel that would benefit the person and the organization.

The second aspect of the primacy of people and relationships in organizations that I will discuss is staff attraction and retention. I will discuss some *ubuntu* values that can be used to improve organizations' staff attraction and retention efforts.

Organizations as Extended Families

Home is where life is found in all its fullness

Home is where life is found in its fullness. The greatest value families offer is that they provide a home. Home is where one feels most contented. Home is where children are born, grow up and become responsible citizens. The family is always present. It is there to welcome one when one arrives in the world. It is also the last to bid farewell when one leaves the world. Home provides the highest sense of belonging. It accords the closest human relationships possible. It is where one's heart is. This is where the saying *Blood is thicker than water* comes from. A healthy family is the greatest life support system.

Healthy families are characterized by:

Shared values – the family has agreed and shared values that are practically lived by all members. The values provide the bond that cements the people together.

Permanency – families are permanent. This is where children are born, grow up, become adults and preferably die. This permanency provides a sense of security which is important for healthy living.

Self-perpetuation – families, because they are made up of human beings, are living systems. Like all living systems, therefore, families are self-perpetuating. When family members die, they are replaced by those who are born. When family members leave home, they are replaced by those who are growing up. In this case families can potentially live for ever.

Care and support – one can always turn to the family and be assured that the family will do its best to provide the care and support they need. In times of joy and sorrow one can always count on the family.

Being accommodative and understanding – family members are ideally supposed to like each other. But they don't have to like each other. While there are shared values, differences are accommodated and people are accepted as they are. Some family members are bad news but that does not disqualify them from being part of the family. This is because *Kinship is like a bone, it does not rot.* Members of the family are tied by destiny. Families will be proud of their best members and bear with their worst members. Most important, the family takes special responsibility for its challenged members because *When a madman walks naked, it's his kinsmen who feel ashamed, not himself.*

The most important characteristic of a healthy family is warm and close relationships. Home is where one's heart is. It is when one feels most secure and least vulnerable. This is the type of organizational environment that is conducive to individual and organizational effectiveness. The above characteristics of a healthy family are also characteristics of an effective team or an organization. The word team was originally used to describe a family or a set of draft animals like oxen, horses or dogs harnessed to pull and work together (Morgan, 1997: 195).

When people come to work they come with their full personhood. They carry the whole of who they are to the workplace just as they also carry the workplace into their homes. Personal issues affecting the person will affect their performance at work just as work issues will affect their home lives. People therefore cannot switch their home life off when they walk to the office, just as they cannot switch work life off when they go home. The implication of this is that organizations must provide meaningful space 'for the personal side' of the people working within them. People should be free in formal and informal ways to share and even disclose some of their personal issues to get the support they need. This reminds me of a colleague who told me of a workmate who just disappeared from work in a foreign country to return to his original country because of 'personal pressure'. He was having family problems and he was also having problems with immigration officials but he never shared all these with the colleagues at work. They became too huge for him to resolve. Another colleague in the same office was facing the same problems and he was formally and informally helped, and his personal problems were resolved.

People in organizations must be encouraged to know each other as people so that they can work together better. I went to an African country on a consultancy assignment that took me some months. In the course of the stay I made friends with a person from that country. We could meet in the evenings and on weekends. When I went back home we continued communicating through e-mail and telephone for quite some time. Then suddenly my friend disappeared. My phones could not get through. My e-mails were not being answered. I talked to a friendly elderly person complaining to her about my lost friend whom 'I knew very well'. Her answer was telling. She told me that I had never known my so called

36

friend because one cannot claim to know somebody without going to their home and meeting in addition to them their spouses, children and relatives. This is what I did not do, I never went to my friend's home. This made me think, how can colleagues at work claim they know each other when they do not know the spouses, children and even relatives of the colleagues? How can they build real team spirit if they do not really know each other? The interesting end of my story is that my friend did resurface after two years and I made a point of visiting his home, meeting his spouse and children and relatives. Now I know him.

The proverb *Do not fight a stranger in darkness because when the lights turn on you may discover he was your brother* teaches the importance of knowing each other. Many conflicts arise because people do not know each other well enough or they do not know each other's motives. The art of communication is to know or understand what the other person is not saying and this is only possible if people know each other. The proverb also teaches that many times people fight because of miscommunication. If they know each other and communicate well they will often discover that they actually want the same thing although they may be approaching it from different angles.

Relationships and team spirit building efforts in an organization

---

Practices

- Regular and full staff meetings
- Staff conference once a year (all staff attending)
- Giving staff space to talk about how they feel
- Meals together e.g. Christmas party, birthday parties
- 'At home week' where everyone is supposed to be at the organization, coupled with learning sessions (may be twice a year)

Bees in a Hive as the Most Effective Family in the World

Bees in the beehive are the most effective 'family' in the world. Bees live in hives with a clear social organization. Each has three types of bees, each with its distinctive work. The queen lays eggs, the male drones fertilize the eggs and the female workers gather food and care for the hive. Each type of bee is adapted for its work. The workers change their duties as their age increases. They start by feeding the larvae; then they ventilate and cool the hive by fanning it with their wings; then they clean the hive, and finally they leave on food expeditions. Bees of different ages carry out all these varied tasks at any one time.

The worker bees' other main duty is to attack and, if necessary, sting intruders. When the worker bee uses her sting, her gut is usually ripped out and she dies soon afterwards. Her defence therefore is an act of suicide in which she sacrifices her life for the other bees.

Social ties hold the bees together. The workers lick both the larvae and the queen when they are not busy working. The workers collect food for everyone in the hive. Worker bees out collecting food pass on messages to tell other bees where to find food. They do this by 'dances'. On returning to the hive from the food source, two kinds of dances may be performed. If the food is less than 100 metres away the bee performs a dance in which it moves round and round telling the other bees food is near but not exactly where to find it. If the food is more than 100 metres away, another dance is performed which tells the other bees exactly where the food is.

What can Organizations Learn?

Bees produce honey, the sweetest substance on earth. They also produce wax, another very useful product. The justification of an organization's existence is determined by how well it is serving the people in its task environment. Organizations must first and foremost produce needed products and services. Non-profit organizations must provided needed services to the people they serve. This is the effective way to ensure an organization's sustainability. Organizations must make a lot of effort to consciously and regularly monitor the relevance of their services and products.

Bees produce two products, honey and wax. Organizations must be focused enough to produce as a few products/services as possible. It is easier to consolidate an organization's identity and create an image when the organization is focused on as a few products or services as possible. When the organization tries to do everything the quality is often compromised.

Just as it is only healthy families than can produce healthy citizens, only healthy organizations can provide health services or products. Organizations that are healthy families are likely to be more effective in service delivery than those that are not.

Leadership – when the hive becomes over crowded, the queen together with some drones and several thousand workers secedes from the colony. The emigrants swarm out to form a new hive. True leaders recognize when their time is up. They move on to give others a chance. Just as in families when children grow up to start their own homes, in healthy organizations leaders have effective succession plans, they mentor the next leaders and move on when their time is up and leave the organization with the least turbulence.

In the old hive meanwhile, the workers remaining behind raise a small batch of the old queen's eggs. The eggs develop into new queens. The first one to emerge immediately searches out the other queen cells and stings their occupants to death. If it so happens that two queens emerge at the same time, they engage in mortal combat until one remains victorious.

The promotion of flat organizations does not mean doing away with positional leadership. There can only be one legitimate leader at a time. Positional leadership must be earned. It must not be given on a silver platter. Organizations must encourage building leadership from within. Bringing in outsiders, while it may have its advantages, may also have serious disadvantages especially if those inside the organization think that the outsiders are not bringing much added value that they can bring themselves.

Structure – in the hive there are three types of bees, each with its different functions. Each type is adapted for its particular job. The division of labour is determined by sex, upbringing and age. The different individuals are accepted and appreciated. Each group in the hive is qualified and experienced and therefore has something to offer to the hive.

Organizations are made up of individuals and teams. It is the different values, skills and experiences that help the organization to work well. Effective organizations need a mix of people able to work well together.

The expectations are very clear in the hive. The drones are expected to fertilize eggs, the queen is expected to lay eggs and the workers are expected to maintain the hive.

Organizations and teams within them will not progress if expectations are not clear. Members must understand and be clear about their roles, their responsibilities and what is expected of them. This reduces the risk of conflict and misunderstanding.

Relationships – bees live together over a long period of time. The bees live and work together well. With clear division of labour in the hive, no bee is forced to work – they work willingly. In the winter, bees cling together in compact masses. The bees in the centre always work their way out; those on the surface work their way in. A clump of bees thereby withstands freezing, even when exposed to very low temperatures.

It may take a long time for individuals and teams within organizations to work well together. Organizations must have strong internal relationships. They need to work closely together to share and discuss ideas and solutions with all members contributing. When conditions get tough relationships need to become even stronger.

In the hive, there is a high degree of support among members. Workers feed the larvae – the weak members. They also attack and, if necessary, sting intruders, sacrificing their lives in the process. They are willing to give up their lives for the wellbeing of the hive.

People in an organization need to support one another. New members may need a lot of support. Belonging to an organization or teams within an organization may call for sacrifices from the members. Being a member in the organization, individuals may be required to change individual values in order to fit in with the values and behaviour of the organization as a whole.

Each individual in the organization must take this responsibility to protect the organization from outside forces, which might destroy it. Individuals need to be committed to the organization's purpose and to one another. This commitment is the force that bonds the individuals together even in adverse conditions.

When they come back from their food expeditions successfully, the worker bees perform dances. Organizations will not be successful without effective communication. Open communication builds trust. Organizations need access to information so that individuals and teams can manage themselves well. Individuals and teams in organizations need to listen to each other.

Successful organizations are fun. Dancing is a sign of celebration, happiness and fun. Individuals get a lot satisfaction by being part of the organization and may openly express excitement, enthusiasm and enjoyment while carrying out their roles and responsibilities.

Every time the workers come back from food expeditions they call for a 'meeting' to give feedback on the success of the trip. Frequent and regular meetings play a critical role in the success of organizations. People in organizations must physically meet and update each other about developments in relation to the task. After the 'meetings' the bees go out together to get the food. Effective organizations get the work done.

Self-development – in its life, a worker bee does not perform the same duties continually. The age of the bee determines the kind of work it can do; the young bees perform housekeeping tasks, the older ones make food collection trips. The middle aged ones spend their time feeding the queen and the younger bees.

Individuals in organizations must grow and develop. As they grow and develop in their skills and competences, so must their responsibilities grow and develop. Flexibility in organizations is a great asset. Varied activities make life more exciting. Organizations and teams that offer little variety may soon lose their appeal.

Bees have clear and meaningful work – producing eggs, caring for the larvae and maintaining the hive. Likewise, organizations need a good a balance between task achievement and maintaining or building up organizational members.

It is also important that individuals must benefit from belonging to the organization. They should gain more than they put into the organization. Individuals must see added value to their efforts in the organization.

Sustainability and efficient use of resources – the workers ensure that the hive has all the practical resources it needs to perform well. The bees that go to collect food gather nectar, which is turned to honey in the hive. The honey is sealed in wax in preparation for winter when there are not as many flowers to provide nectar.

Organizations must think about not only short-term but also long-term resource needs. They should consciously seek to become self-reliant in the long term. This is the essence of organizational sustainability.

When winter is approaching all the drones are expelled from the colony. Not contributing to the wellbeing of the population makes the males merely use up food, which is at a premium in the cold season.

In addition to acquiring more resources, organizations must seek to make efficient use of the resources they already have. Many organizations do not maximize the use of the resources they have. There is a lot of waste. A good example is in information technology. Many organizations, for example, use the computer only as a typewriter and adding machine.

Relationships with stakeholders – Bees have mutually beneficial relationships with stakeholders. While they take nectar from the flowers, they simultaneously aid in the pollination process of the plants.

According to the Associated Press (2008) in the US alone bee pollination is responsible for $15 billion in crop value.

Organizations must seek to add value to any relationships that they commit to, and at the same time they must see to it that all the relationships they get involved in are adding value to them and not taking value away. This is the principle of synergy. Any relationship not adding value is not worth maintaining.

The above sections have discussed some of the critical organizational success factors we can learn from the family of bees in a hive. Bees in a hive are the most effective family and organization in the world. The critical success factors are focus and concentration; leadership, structure, internal relationships, self-development, sustainability; and relationships with stakeholders. The most important thing however is that the bees act as a family or a team.

Staff Attraction and Retention

The failure to attract and retain staff and the consequent problem of staff turnover is a universal problem (Suzuki, 1998: 196, 197). High staff turnover is a major hindrance to organizational effectiveness among most organizations. Working as a consultant to non-profit organizations, I am often surprised by how much organizations change within a period of three years. One study we conducted indicated that 50% of the professional staff stayed in their organizations for an average of 18 months before moving on to other organizations (Malunga, 2003). This theoretically means that the organization 'starts all over again' every three years. The people who left the organizations were mostly professional and technical staff. Those who left the organizations least were directors and non-professional staff. Visiting these organizations after three years one can hardly recognize the new people there, except perhaps for the directors and very junior staff. The problem of staff turnover is reaching alarming proportions in many non-profit organizations.

In the study referred to above, the reasons given by directors for staff leaving their organizations included: looking for greener pastures, increased demand for professional employees on the labour market, uncertainty of funding and therefore job security, and lack of a career progression path in the organization.

The reasons given by the professional staff themselves included: inadequate salaries and benefits, relationship problems with leaders, work not challenging enough, lack of a career progression path in the organization, non-facilitative policies, systems and procedures, and job insecurity.

The reasons given by those professional staff who actually left their organizations included: perceived unfair treatment by leaders, relationship problems with leaders, rigid structures and policies, low levels of responsibility, no staff development, and false participation – 'involving us when decisions had already been made'.

The reasons given by the directors placed more emphasis on salaries and benefits, and opportunities for personal growth. The reasons for staff turnover given by the professional staff tended more towards higher factors of relationships, values, visions and missions. Those who had actually left their organizations gave reasons that tended towards the need for more power sharing in their previous organizations. Most of these had moved to more senior positions in their new organizations. Surprisingly none of them mentioned low pay as a reason for moving from their previous organizations.

From the reasons given above we can develop a model for staff turnover in organizations:

Fig 3.1 Staff turnover model

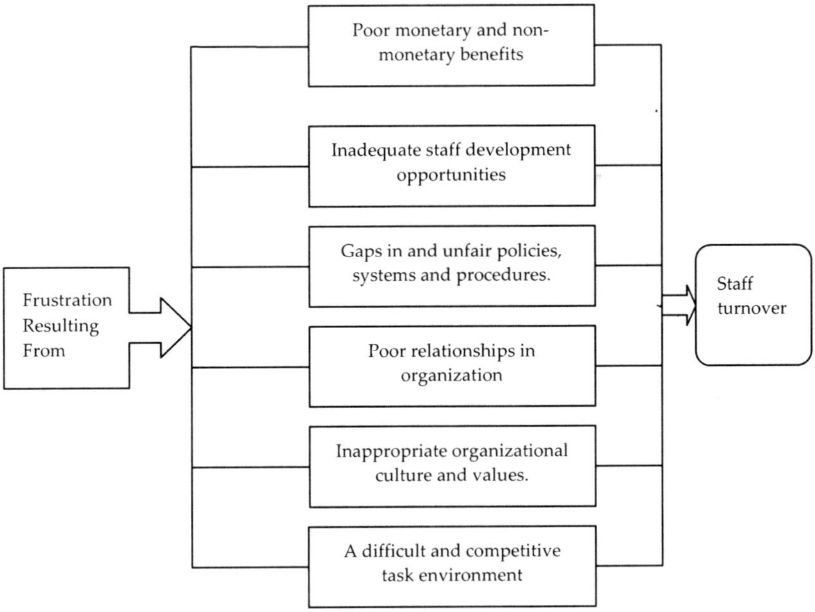

Source: author

Effects of Staff Turnover

While staff turnover is not entirely negative in that it has some positive elements – like gains through new staff bringing in new ideas, innovations, best practices which may be a terrific source of improvement for the organization, and perhaps cheaper than costly staff development – staff turnover beyond certain levels always is detrimental to the organization that staff are leaving. Staff turnover or the failure to attract and retain staff has a number of negative effects on an organization. Among these are:

Loss of organizational memory – when key staff leave, they leave with their knowledge, experience and expertise. This is aggravated in situations where organizations do not have effective knowledge management systems.

Loss of organizational morale – organizational relationships and bonds are disrupted. Sometimes those who leave are seen as heroes, creating envy and suffocating morale in those remaining behind. This undermines their commitment to the organization's future.

Hindered organizational development and growth – an organization is only as strong as the people it employs and their continued stay in the organization. According to Vincent (1995: 375) it takes a minimum of 10 years of undisturbed and concerted organizational effort for a non-profit organization to become reasonably sustainable. When staff keep moving at a rapid rate, the organization may never become sustainable and effective.

Increased costs – losing an employee can cost the organization between 40% and 60% of the individual's annual salary (Hamylin, 1996: 43). If organizations lose up to 50% of their staff in three years the costs can be quite high. In addition to financial costs, loss of key personnel may lead to low organizational effectiveness as new people coming to replace them may bring with them different and sometimes contradictory values (Bulhungu, 1999: 55).

Rapid turnover of staff limits the ability of the organization to start building a foundation of knowledge and experience from which to draw future learning and on which to build an increasingly competent and rigorous body of practice (Taylor, 2001: 18).

Improving Staff Attraction and Retention

The directors, professional staff, and the staff who had actually left their organizations had some suggestions on how the problem could be resolved. Directors had the following suggestions: better packages (loans and better salaries); long term core funding to reduce fear and anxiety about job insecurity; improved policies, systems and procedures, having a clear development path for the professional staff; and an effective recruitment system.

Professional staff had the following suggestions: better packages (salaries, medical, housing, transport and educational allowances), improved working relationships, improved policies, systems and procedures to ensure fairness, and improved leadership styles. They also suggested introducing staff development, ensuring sustainable funding and making the decision making process more inclusive.

Professional staff who had left their organizations made the following suggestions: ensuring effective succession plans, removing bureaucratic processes, involving professional staff to ensure organizational ownership, and building an atmosphere of trust. They also suggested that to address the problem of staff turnover the organization should commit itself to employee job security and improve negotiation skills with donors and sponsors for sustainable core funding

The emphasis of the directors' solutions is on acquiring more material resources, improving skills and competences and improving policies, systems and procedures. Except for the need for better packages and the need to ensure sustainable funding, the professional staff's solutions emphasized the values of the organization, working relationships, leadership styles and participation. The solutions are crystallized in the reasons given by the staff who actually left their organizations; these emphasized issues of organizational culture, values and relationships in addressing the problem.

Most non-profit organizations do not conduct conscious exit interviews when staff leave. They therefore do not have conscious systems to enable them to reflect on the problem so as to find corrective measures. Most directors have a feeling that the organizations where members who leave find new jobs are better than theirs. This makes them feel that the problem of staff turnover is inevitable and that staff attraction and retention is a difficult if not impossible task.

Most members of staff have a feeling that 'there is a better organization out there' and they are looking forward to getting out of their current organization to find the 'ideal organization'. The attitude of working to make the current organization to become the desired organization is usually absent. The general attitude among staff is that making the organization 'inhabitable and therefore able to retain staff' is the responsibility of the few leaders at the top. They therefore abdicate all responsibility to the leaders.

It is interesting to note the shift that took place among a group of leaders who went through a workshop facilitated by the author to discuss how organizations can improve their staff and attraction and retention. When asked at the beginning of the workshop about the main causes of staff turnover in their organizations, they identified lack of funding, lack of staff development opportunities, and job insecurity. At the end of the workshop, when asked the same question, they identified lack of a clear and shared vision, a restrictive rather than empowering culture, and a gap between management and the board. This means that going through the workshop, they were able to make a shift from lower to higher levels of organizational consciousness. This shift among the leaders is indispensable in improving staff attraction and retention in a sustainable manner.

From the reasons given above, a model of staff attraction and retention can be developed.

Fig 3.2 Staff attraction and retention model

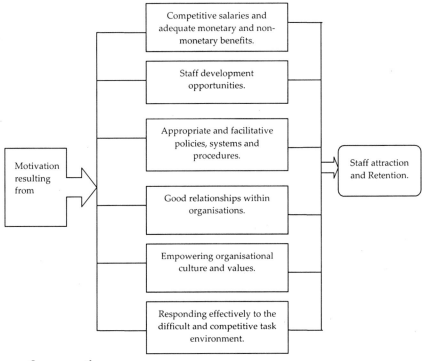

Source: author

Ubuntu Contribution to Staff Attraction and Retention

Two proverbs illustrate ubuntu values that can help in an organization's staff attraction and retention efforts. These are: A wise man marries the woman he loves; a wiser man loves the woman he marries and A beautiful girl does not need to be a great dancer.

Lack of contentment is characteristic of human beings. Grass always looks greener on the other side. People work very hard to get what they want and when they get it they wonder if they really needed it in the first place. The search for the next similar thing begins. A wise man marries the woman he loves; a wiser man loves the woman he marries. The proverb is a lesson in contentment. It teaches that before making a commitment one has many options and choices. After commitment the choices and options are reduced. Instead of opting out, which may be the easier route when the going gets tough, one ought to work at making the commitment work. Marriages are supposed to be permanent. There is only one expected option: love the person you are married to. The proverb further teaches the importance of marrying the person one loves because it will be easier to remain committed. It teaches against the thinking that 'I will learn to love this person after I am married to them'. People must make commitments to things, organizations and causes that they are passionate about. This will sustain their commitment after the decision has been taken. In conclusion, it must be noted that it is easier to love before commitment but much harder to continue loving with same fervour after the decision has been taken and reality has taken the place of infatuation.

A beautiful girl does not need to be a great dancer. Human interactions are about attraction. People are either attracted to us or repelled. People are rarely neutral. There are two ways of attracting attention. Metaphorically, these are 'beauty' and 'great dancing'. A beautiful girl attracts by her beauty. She attracts by grace. She attracts simply by being. In contrast, a great dancer like the African traditional masquerade dancers attracts by doing something. He attracts by dancing. A related proverb is If you are ugly you must learn to dance.

In attracting and retaining staff, both organizations and individuals have obligations. Individuals have the obligation to 'love the organizations' they are married to, or make their organizations the best they can be, rather than opting out to greener pastures. Institutions have an obligation to become 'beautiful' so that the staff will continue being wooed and faithful.

The proverb A wise man marries the woman he loves; a wiser man loves the woman he marries challenges staff to love their organizations. It challenges them to commit to contribute towards making their organizations the ideal organization that people would otherwise be seeking elsewhere. In the words of Robert Collier, it encourages them to 'start where you are, distant fields always look greener but opportunity lies right where you are'. While the staff are following their obligation to love the organization they are married to, the leadership is challenged to cultivate organizational beauty so that the organization can attract and retain the staff. A beautiful girl does not need to be a great dancer. Great dancing in this case means concentrating on the lower organizational aspects of salaries and training opportunities. In other words, it means concentrating on what organizations can do for staff. It means concentrating on the organization's doing. Cultivating beauty means concentrating on higher organizational aspects: relationships among colleagues and with superiors, leadership styles, culture and values, and consciously linking individuals and organizations' visions, missions and strategies. In other words it means concentrating on cultivating a beautiful organizational culture or on the being of the organization. In short a beautiful organization is one that is responsive to employee needs or is perceived to be doing its best to be responsive to those needs under the circumstances. It is a humane organization, or it has a human face. Investing in cultivating organizational beauty is the sustainable way of improving the organizational staff attraction and retention. It is the way of sustaining the staff's love for the organization.

Conclusion

Just like any other model, the model of bees in a hive as family and organization has its limitations. A major limitation is that the activities in the hive are instinctual and unconscious. Coincidentally, this is a similar limitation in many organizations. Organizational consciousness is low in many organizations. This is a major explanation of why people in organization spend more energy in improving programme and project activities than in addressing organizational issues holistically. While instinct may be sufficient for bees, organizations that are not consciously improving themselves cannot be effective and sustainable in the long term.

Despite its limitations, we can learn a lot about organizations from the example of bees as a family. The bees have managed to realize the proverb *Home is where life is found in its fullness.* Since we spend most of our waking hours at our workplace, workplaces are in fact the second if not the only homes for some people. The challenge is to truly turn them from being merely offices to 'homes' or families. Organizations must be viewed as extended families in which relationships are close enough to go beyond the professional level. People must be free to interfere in each other's lives both inside and outside the organization, especially if such interference would benefit the organization and the person concerned.

As seen from the metaphor of the bees, the concept of organizations as extended families or the caring organization should not imply a stagnant or staff serving organization. To the contrary, the caring organization should be seen as a prerequisite for a mission serving and highly performing organization, because happy staff and volunteers will mean happy clients and customers.

Many non-profit organizations do not pay their staff as much as private corporations do. They therefore have a lot of challenges in ensuring the loyalty of the staff. Many of them have initiatives aimed at enhancing staff loyalty such as: increased maternity and paternity leave, subsidized bus or train fares to and from the office, longer annual leave and subsidies for staff professional development efforts. These are however usually faced with such problems as bad communication, people not knowing about these provisions, and unfair allocation of the opportunities. The practice of *ubuntu* values of transparency, fairness and brotherhood or sisterhood would go a long way in adding value to these efforts.

The proverbs *A wise man marries the woman he loves; a wiser man loves the woman he marries* and *A beautiful girl does not need to be a great dancer* illustrate the *ubuntu* values that would help organizations in their staff attraction and retention efforts. Staff need to show commitment to their organizations. Organizational leaders need to create conducive environments that encourage the staff to commit to the organization. Staff turnover cannot be entirely eliminated but these efforts would help to keep it at manageable levels.

Finally, the proverb *It is better to be surrounded by people than to be surrounded by things* teaches the importance and relationships over things: the importance of personal communication and face to face meetings, especially when these can serve better than impersonal and written communication. The proverb teaches the value of human contact. It emphasizes the importance of consciously creating more humane rather than mechanical organizations.

Adopting Family Values for Organizational Effectiveness

Reflect on the questions below:

- What makes bees in a hive an effective family and organization?
- How similar is this model to our organization?
- How different is it from our organization?
- What could we do differently to become a more effective organization?

How can we use the lessons from the beehive model to become more family like as an organization?

How well does our organization express the following family values?

Rate 0 – 5 0 = non-existent, 5 = excellent

Organizational family like value	Rate 0 - 5	Explanation
• Shared values among staff		
• A sense of permanency		
• Self-perpetuating and continuous improvement capacity (capacity of organization to survival beyond current staff)		
• Care and support		
• Being accommodative to diversity and demonstrating understanding to staff needs		
• Warm and close relationships		

Which traits is our organization strong on? Which ones is it weak on? What should be done to make the organization more family like and a home?

Staff Attraction and Retention Assessment Tool

Rate 0 – 5 0 = non – existent, 5 = excellent

How well do the following elements support staff attraction and retention in your organization?

Element	Rate	Explanation
• Organizational culture and values		
• Leadership styles		
• Organizational strategy		
• Relationships with superiors		
• Relationships among staff		
• Organizational structure		
• Support to self-development		
• Learning systems		
• Exit interviews		
• Policies, systems and procedures (financial, human resources and administrative)		
• Staff development practices		
• Salaries and benefits		

From the above rating what are the strengths and limitations of our staff attraction and retention systems and practices? What do we need to do to build on the strengths and address the limitations?

•

Reflection Proverbs

What can we learn about the importance of people and relationships in organizations from the following proverbs?

It is better to be surrounded by people than to be surrounded by things

Home is where life is found in its fullness

When a mad person walks naked, it is his or her kinsmen who feel ashamed, not himself or herself

A wise man marries the woman he loves, a wiser man loves the woman he marries

A beautiful girl does not need to be a great dancer

How can we use the lessons from these proverbs to improve team spirit and commitment in the organization?

Chapter 4

PARTICIPATORY LEADERSHIP AND DECISION MAKING

If you want to arrive fast go alone, if you want to arrive far go with others

Introduction

In this chapter, I will discuss some of the myths and realities of participatory leadership and decision making in organizations. I will then discuss some lessons organizations can learn on participatory leadership and decision making from *ubuntu* cultures. The chapter is based on the proverb *If you want to arrive fast go alone but if you want to arrive far go with others*.

Whilst writing this chapter, I took a break to attend a live Dionne Warwick concert at the New Theater Hall in Oxford. I thoroughly enjoyed the show but most importantly I validated the idea that leadership is a performing art. Leadership stripped to its bare essentials is about three things: the leader, the followers and a vision or destination where the leader and followers want to travel together to and this is what I saw at the concert: Dionne Warwick- the musician, the entertainer and the leader, the audience- the followers and her performance – the promise and the vision. Sitting through the concert, a few leadership insights came to my mind. First her presence – she didn't need to do anything. It was enough that she was there. Then her voice –it was crispy, deep and almost seductive. It was clear and engaging. It was sweet to listen to. It wasn't all about singing (the work she came to do). The songs were interspersed with one continuous story – the story of her life – how she came to be the Dionne Warwick who was on stage that night. She did not rush from one song to another. By telling her story she may not have *gone fast* - singing many songs but she managed to *arrive further* – by travelling together with the audience through her story. It was also about the self-confidence – the idea of being comfortable with oneself and who one is that she exuded to the audience. She is 67 and she has 6 grand children but she is still a girl and she looks and feels like one. In addition to all these I thought it went beyond what she was singing, how she was singing to how she made the audience feel. She made me feel like I was the only one in the audience and that she was performing personally for me. Lastly, it was about the brand, the uniqueness built upon and cultivated upon a solid track-record. Towards the end she introduced the band members personally to the audience one by one. She said they were the real architect of the successful Dionne Warwick brand which she herself was only a part of.

I left feeling I knew her and that she knew me. Did I know her? Was it important that I did or I did not? I guess the most important thing is that I was satisfied. The show was worthy my money, my time and my attention. I got into a taxi feeling what a memorable moment the show was! I guess that is the destination Dionne Warwick wanted to travel with her audience to. And it was all participatory.

According to Professor John Hailey (personal communication), leadership is by nature participatory and the term 'participatory leadership' is redundant. Leadership that is not to any extent participatory may not be described as leadership in the true sense of the word. But there are some myths about participatory leadership which, if they are not separated from realities, may inhibit effective practice of leadership in organizations. Most organizations have embraced the notion of participatory leadership and decision making but the practice of the concept in most organizations lags behind its theory. I am surprised that the more we write and read and talk about leadership, the more effective leaders and leadership seem to be in short supply. There is no organizational topic that has been given as much attention as the topic of leadership. I believe part of the explanation of this paradox is that we have not been able to separate the myths and realities of effective leadership.

Myths and Realities of Participatory Leadership and Decision Making in Organizations

According to the *Oxford Dictionary*, a myth is an idea that forms part of the beliefs of a group but is not founded on fact. Reality refers to something that exists or that is real. Separating myths from realities enables people to base their decisions on facts rather than imaginary illusions.

Myth no 1: Participatory leadership and decision making mean the same thing to all people in the organization

The word participation strikes a natural chord in most people. Most people agree with the notion of participation. Since participation is a generally agreed concept few people feel the need to define it and clarify what it means in their particular organizational context. Because of this lack of clarity people may assume they are talking about the same thing when in fact they may not.

Reality: Participatory leadership and decision making may mean different things to different people.

Participatory leadership and decision making may mean democracy, consultation or consensus. Democracy means voting with the majority winning and the minority losing. A typical example is how board meetings deal with consent agendas. It also means that 'our leaders will represent us at the meetings we cannot attend'.

In consultation, the leaders ask for opinions from the staff and then at the end make a decision 'after hearing from all sides'. The leaders actively take full responsibility of the decisions taken.

In consensus the leader and followers sit down and talk until all views have been exhausted and a meeting of the minds has been reached. A mutually agreeable decision is arrived at.

The challenge that comes from the myth that participatory leadership and decision making mean the same thing is that typically most leaders want consultation while most staff want consensus. Staff therefore may see their leaders as not being participatory enough or actually as being dictators, while the leaders may see their staff as dragging them towards 'participation paralysis' which may arise out of seeking consensus. In addition many leaders are happy to consult and sometimes even to build consensus but expect the outcome to agree with the decisions they would have made on their own. An example that comes to mind is a president who went to court to ask for an interpretation of a particular section of the constitution. Apparently, he had his own preferred interpretation. When the court gave an interpretation he was not happy with, he refused to take the court's interpretation. Few leaders have the humility to ask the staff or volunteers to 'defend their point and be willing to change their original position if the facts clearly prove the need for this'.

A corollary to this is the belief in the fallacy of 'over-participation' as illustrated by a pastor I interviewed who said:

> If I as a leader I am to start a church by asking people what the church should do for them, and I start the church based on what they want, I will grow a big church very fast. I will let the person, the culture and the environment dictate the very nature of this new church.

> There is another 'better' way to start a church. It is to find out what God wants the church to be. No matter what culture, no matter what the time, no matter what the interests of the people I serve, and even no

matter personal preferences, I need to first be clear on what God wants the church to be.

Once I am anchored in His principles, his voice and values and I go to the people and ask them, 'what are you looking for in a church?' then we can get creative and respond to their needs without compromising God's vision for the church.

This illustrates that the leader has the ultimate responsibility for the vision; anyone who does not is not a leader. Participatory leadership does not necessarily mean asking people what the vision is or should be. It is helping them to buy into the vision.

Myth no.2: One type of participation is better than the other

Leaders, because of their natural tendency towards consultation, and staff, because of their natural tendency towards consensus, may be tempted to feel that either consultation or consensus is a better way of expressing the spirit of participation in the organization. When faced with difficult issues both groups may feel the best way is to cast a vote, preferably in a secret ballot.

Reality: There is no one right way of participation

There is no one right way of participation that works well all the time. Two of the factors that come into play are the group involved and the type of decisions to be made. A highly empowered group may do well with consensus, while a not so empowered group may do well with less participatory modes and using consensus with this group may lead only to participation paralysis. Decisions that will need the support of many will need more participation while those that do not may not require similar levels of participation. A re-engineering process will require higher levels of consensus, as compared to a decision to fire an individual, for example.

Myth no. 3: Leaders can easily switch from one participation orientation to another

It is usually assumed that a leader who has been successful in one organization or department will also be successful in another. We see non-profit organization leaders, for example, switching to politics and making a big success on the basis of their experience in the non-profit sector. We also see others who flounder or who seem to have 'lost their bearings'. The same happens to leaders who move from one organization to another or even from one department to another.

Reality: Different situations may demand different forms of participation

Many leaders are comfortable with a particular form of participation or leadership style. A leader may be comfortable with consultation when the situation demands that he or she may need to use democracy, consensus or even autocracy. A key point of leadership development must be self-knowledge in what forms of leadership styles one is comfortable with and likely to be biased towards, how to develop capacity for other forms of leadership styles so that one can be flexible when the situation so demands.

Myth no. 4: Participatory leadership is always good and autocratic leadership is always bad

There is a strong feeling that participatory leadership of whatever type is always good and autocratic leadership is always bad. Leadership is about rallying people to a better future. But in any change process resistance is normal and it is to be expected. What is good for many may not necessarily be good for all. Some have different vested interests and they defend these interests. In this case one will observe that participatory leadership may have a shadow in the sense that those wishing to defend their interests may use it to slow down and if possible stop change. Too many meetings that do not end in anything concrete is an example.

Reality: Even in a culture of participation, there is room for some beneficial autocracy

Even in a culture of participatory leadership and decision making there is a place for autocratic action if the situation demands it. The ability to take such action may be a measure of the strength of leadership. When people overrule the unreasonable wishes of a dead person's will, or when they override a child's will in terms of getting medication critical to that child's health and life, they are not being participatory with the dead person or the child, but they are being responsible.

Participatory leadership and decision making may be used to avoid taking responsibility or making difficult decisions as leaders when the situation requires one to do so. This reminds me of an organization in which there was a conflict between a manager who was trying to introduce new technology to the organization and an employee who was supplying the then current technology that the organization was using. This employee was actually seconded to the organization to manage the technology. He resisted every move the manager was taking to introduce new technology. The manager reported this to his supervisors but nothing happened as the supervisors did not want to disappoint both the manager and the employee from the other company. They kept having many 'participatory meetings to hear from both sides' with no clear decision made. The conflict dragged on and on and by the time the old technology was replaced the organization had lost much in time, money and perceived integrity of the leadership. Many organizations have failed to stop projects that are no longer needed, or to fire people who are no longer needed, even to discipline staff, in the name of 'participatory leadership and decision making'. The point is that participatory leadership and decision-making should not mean avoiding responsibility or giving guidance where there is a deadlock and a decision needs to be made. Participatory leadership should not mean buying time and wasting time when the course of action is clear and obvious.

Myth no. 5: Participatory and autocratic leadership and decision making are mutually exclusive

It is believed that since participatory leadership brings ideas and contributions from all, the decisions made and subsequent action taken are superior to those that would follow from an autocratic process. It is also generally believed that participatory leadership and decision making cannot take place in 'autocratic' organizations.

Reality: Participation may bring inefficiency as it slows down action

Participation will only bring synergy if the ideas sought are 'worth their salt'. This therefore limits the people to participating according to the usefulness of their ideas and the value those ideas will add to the ends sought. The idea of universal participation is a fallacy. We can only have limited participation, beyond which we may begin to experience what the economists would call a 'diminishing rate of returns' where each additional participation actually takes away the value and cost-effectiveness of the decision to be made. A typical challenge in many organizations is too many meetings where everyone is supposed to attend in the name of participation. Meetings would be more helpful if we had the least number of them with only the critical people to attend. The rest can be informed about what transpired at the meeting and if they happen to have brilliant ideas they may bring them up before the meeting or as feedback to the meeting reports. This would improve efficiency and free a lot of time for other useful commitments. Many organizations suffer from the problem of 'more meetings than work'.

There may be need for a balance of the two to reach an optimum speed for getting things done. Participatory decision making takes a long time for the process, with hopefully shorter time for implementation. Top-down decision making is short on process but much time is needed to correct and redirect consensus during implementation. Both ways take about the same amount of time, but organizations have not yet developed patience for the former, with the push for results and 'rapid start up'. Sometimes they suffer from 'participation paralysis' and nothing moves. Smillie and Hailey (2001: 131) concluded from their study of South Asian non-profits that hierarchy and participatory management could be compatible and complementary.

Myth no. 6: Decentralization leads to more participatory leadership and decision making in an organization

I have been involved in a number of restructuring interventions for NGOs and non-profit organizations in Europe which are decentralizing or creating field offices in the developing regions of the world with the aim of 'increasing participation' of the people in developing countries. It is assumed that setting up field offices will increase participation and decision making.

Reality: Decentralization does not necessarily mean participation

Decentralization describes the degree to which authority and responsibility are spread down and outwards within an organization. There are three forms of decentralization: deconcentration, delegation and devolution. Deconcentration simply means the transfer of some tasks from headquarters to field offices with all authority remaining with headquarters. Delegation is the allocation of authority to field offices. Devolution is the transfer of authority to individuals and groups that are independent of the organization – this is the deepest level of decentralization.

Decentralization is not the same as participation. A highly centralized organization may use participatory techniques to get contributions from senior managers (Smillie and Hailey, 2001: 131). An organization may simply 'deconcentrate' its management without giving the field offices any real authority for meaningful participation. Participatory processes will probably make decentralization more effective.

In summary, leadership is by its very essence participatory in nature but it is important to separate the myths and realities of participatory leadership and decision making. This separation will greatly improve the practical relevance of the concept of participatory leadership and decision making. Participation means different things to different people; no one leadership style is better than another; leaders tend to have natural tendencies that make them biased and therefore more effective in some styles and not others. Decentralization will only make participatory sense if moves beyond deconcentration. Finally, participatory leadership is not always good and autocratic leadership is not always bad.

One of the reasons why the myths of participatory leadership and decision making persist in organizations is that most organizations pay only lip service to the notion. To show commitment organizations need to invest in the development of the people's leadership capacity. Bennis and Thomas (2002: 171) report that investing in staff improves their 'participatory capacity'. They observe that a 10% increase spending on leadership development pushes productivity up by 8.5%. To prove that they are experience, organizations must put their money where their mouth is.

Participatory Leadership and Decision Making in *Ubuntu* Cultures

Mangaliso (2001: 27) observed that many Western decision making processes are linear in nature or involve a conscious choice of action from available alternatives. They involve problem definition, determination of causes of the problem, generation of alternative solutions and implementation of the chosen alternative. In contrast, in *ubuntu* cultures problem solving is circular as opposed to linear. It is inclusive and may move at a much slower speed because those who have different views are given opportunity to present their point of view. A decision reached by consensus therefore is more valued than the decision that may be reached by voting in non-*ubuntu* cultures.

At first glance, indigenous African leadership appears automatic and autocratic, and although some were born in the royal lineage, the approval of the people was critical for the legitimacy of newly elected leaders.

The accountability of leaders was reinforced because there were many possible candidates for leadership, so that strict criteria were applied to determine who would emerge as a leader. This decision was often subject to the approval of the people. Responsibility was a major determining factor because it was believed that *No matter how blunt, a machete should never be held by a mad person.*

As Professor Michongwe explains (2005, personal communication), to emerge as a leader candidates had to show competence in understanding people and human nature, understanding human relationships, conflicts and how to manage them, diplomacy and relationships with other kingdoms, the art of war, strategic thinking, and kingdom secrets and how to guard them.

As noted earlier, Nelson Mandela (1994: 20) describes the profound influence that the democratic decision-making processes of the Tembu people (of which his grandfather was chief) had on him. While a king in Africa was the most visible leader and the indigenous custodian of power, auxiliary authorities – often people of highly respected religious or elder status – continually advised the king in roles that promoted democracy in the kingdom. Tangwa (1998:2) observed that while the king generally appeared very powerful from outside, he or she was nevertheless subject to very strict control, not only by means of taboos, but also from institutions and personalities whose main occupation was the protection and safeguarding of the people, the ancestors, the land and the unborn. Indigenous leadership, therefore, did not consist solely of the authority of the ruler, but was influenced by queen mothers, godfathers, councils, secret societies, mystics, rituals, ceremonies, rules and citizens. The king's decisions were continually subject to review by others (Mologtlegi, 2004:3).

As described earlier, a council of elders often played a key leadership role in the kingdom through the following roles and responsibilities. It practiced a values-based leadership style. Values-based leadership is a values-driven, change oriented and a developmental style of leadership. The purpose of this style of leadership is to help team members to change and grow in order to become proactive contributors to the community or the organization. It makes it possible to create a values-laden culture in the organization by providing for equal participation in decision making, support for risk taking, confronting of change and developing of a sense of community among the members; conveying passion and strong emotional conviction; and instilling values which generate a sense of belonging and belief in the goals among the members. (Poovan and Engelbrecht, 2006: 20)

Roles and Responsibilities of the Board

The equivalent of the council of elders in modern organizations is the board. In addition to being a legal requirement, the board has five key roles and responsibilities. (Tandon, 1995: 42).

Being custodians of the organization

The control of the organization rests with the board. In non-profit organizations, the board represents the voluntary nature of the organization in the sense that board membership is voluntary and non-paid while staff are paid. They are also the custodians of the vision, mission and values of the organization.

Key responsibilities of the board in this regard include: ensuring that the organization is registered, ensuring that it is true to its vision, mission and values, ensuring that it is legal and ethical all the time; and taking ultimate responsibility of success and failure of the organization.

Mission

It is the responsibility of the board to set the vision and mission of the organization. Vision refers to what the organization would want to see changed in society as a result of its work, while mission concerns the organization's identity, purpose, constituency and operating values. The vision properly formulated, communicated and shared by many is the strongest engine propelling the organization into its desired future. It is the ultimate guide to all organizational decisions.

The key responsibilities of the board in regard to the mission are: ensuring that the organization has a clear mission statement, reviewing the mission statement regularly to reflect changes in the task environment, encouraging feedback and comments on the mission statement from staff and other stakeholders, and promoting the mission statement to as many stakeholders as possible. In short the responsibility of the board is to foresee the future and prepare the organization for it (Kemp, 1990: 16).

Oversight

This means establishing checks and balances to avoid abuse. This includes legal, ethical and fiduciary responsibilities including board/staff relationships. A key oversight issue is the avoidance of conflict of interest. A principle regarding this is that all conflict of interest must at best be avoided or at least declared.

As an oversight process the board should periodically commission evaluations and impact assessments in order to know how the organization is doing. In addition to programme assessment it is important that the board must assess the directors against clear and agreed goals. Not only must the board assess others, it must also assess itself as a board and as individual members of the board. The key responsibilities of the board in oversight include leading in the strategic plan processes, and commissioning annual organizational assessments to determine the organization's capacity in terms of financial and material resources, skills and competences, policies, system and procedures, structure, strategy, vision and mission, culture and values, relationships with stakeholders and programme delivery. The responsibilities also include reinforcing the code of ethics among board members and staff, ensuring healthy board/staff relationships, assessing the directors and offering appropriate support, and conducting periodical board assessments.

Many times the board is the last to know that things are not going well in the organization. This is often due to the negligence of its oversight responsibility.

Financial sustainability

Ensuring that the organization has adequate financial and human resources is a major responsibility of the board. Ensuring the organization's financial sustainability is the board's responsibility; it can only be delegated to staff but it is the responsibility of the board. If a non-profit organization closes because there are no funds, it is the board that has failed. Organizations get more credibility from donors and sponsors when their boards take an active role in fundraising because they are assured that since the board plays an oversight function, their money will be well taken care of. And since board members are volunteers, the donors and sponsors know that self-interest cannot be the driving factor in their fundraising efforts.

The key responsibilities of the board in financial sustainability include formulating a financial sustainability plan, monetary contributions or contributions in kind by board members to the organization, identifying members with expertise in organizational sustainability issues, approving and monitoring the annual operating budget, and ensuring independent annual audits.

Public relations

The board must make the organization's mission, values and programmes known to all the organization's stakeholders. This is usually done through reaching out to communities and potential donors. It requires a conscious and systematic approach.

The board's key responsibilities in public relations include scanning the task environment, listening to what stakeholders want or need – particularly important because *There is more wisdom in listening than in speaking* – bringing these to the attention of the board and staff, and ensuring the organization has an effective public relations and marketing strategy. The responsibilities also include identifying and targeting strategic people and institutions who need to know about the organization, ensuring support for organizational policies, and encouraging the building of a positive image of the organization.

Organizational Leadership Challenges

The leadership role in organizations is a shared function between the board and management. In many non-profit organizations, however, relationships between the board and the management are characterized by tension. I worked in an organization where the relationship between the board and management was so tense that the suggested solution was to divide the organization into two. The board was going to recruit new staff and the staff were going to recruit a new board.

The tension in such situations often results from different expectations between the board and management, or from either the management or the board not being fully involved in planning, or from ineffective communication between the board and the management, and ineffective accountability systems, leading to both the board and the management not knowing how they or the other party are performing the duties. This leads to speculation, mistrust and loss of respect.

In the case mentioned above, the board had the idea that the organization should be a 'school' training people who wanted to become consultants, while management had the idea that the organization was a 'consultancy firm' and thought that turning it into a school would only mean creating competition for themselves. The board had gone through a strategic planning process in which they came up with their 'school' vision. Management was not involved in that strategic planning process. Selling the 'school' ideal to management was futile. The main form of communication between the board and management was through memos and reports which, because of the suspicion that had been building up over a long period of time, were mostly misunderstood and only served to build more tension. Finally, because the 'vision' – therefore, what the organization was supposed to be doing – was not shared and agreed, and there was also a lack of interaction and ineffective communication between the board and management, performance measures were not clear. Both the management and the board did not know how to measure the performance of the other. This led to more speculation, mistrust and loss of respect. The result was that the organization finally disintegrated.

How Ubuntu Leadership Practices can Help Modern Organizations

Using the roles and responsibilities of the board and the case presented above, a few lessons may be drawn from the *ubuntu* practice of leadership. These include:

The importance of clear roles and responsibilities. This helps to set boundaries which must be respected – *If the sun says it is more powerful than the moon, then let it come and shine at night* and *The cat in his house has the teeth of a lion.* Related to this is the importance of measuring leadership results on the basis of clear criteria. This is another lesson from *ubuntu* culture. For individuals to be entrusted with leadership they had to demonstrate certain competencies like: understanding people and human nature; understanding human relationships, conflicts and how to manage them; diplomacy and relationships with other kingdoms; the art of war; strategic thinking; and kingdom secrets and how to guard them. This made the level of performance expected from them clear. Organizations need to come up with clear criteria on the competencies they need in their leaders and also the performance levels and quality expected from them and how these will be measured.

Appointments for organizational leadership need to be done with complete transparency and accountability. The process must leave stakeholders satisfied.

Individual leaders or groups should not be allowed to become too powerful. Organizations must have checks and balances that are actually adhered to.

It is important to always ensure meaningful and realistic participation. In other words organizations must separate the myths and realities of participatory leadership and decision making.

As part of participatory leadership, *ubuntu* teaches the importance of face to face meetings and 'difficult dialogue' if need be as a way of creating understanding between groups. Mangaliso (2001: 23) recounts an incident in South Africa where workers had a dispute with management. The workers invited top management to publicly address them on their concerns. The management however turned down their request and instead responded through written statements posted on bulletin boards.

This led to frustration among the staff who then decided to go on a strike that lasted for over two weeks, resulting heavy losses in money and many employees losing their jobs. The strike and subsequent losses would have been avoided if the management had only heeded the request and addressed the employees. In *ubuntu* culture face to face meetings are a sign of respect and care. The leaders had failed to see this and the heavy losses resulted. Organizations need to create space and time to talk. They need to create non-threatening spaces for dialogue.

Another key leadership lesson from the council elders' roles and responsibilities is the importance of planning leadership succession. Organizations must plan for succession in good time, and have a clear and effective system for identifying their successors. The successors must undergo well thought through programmes that will prepare them to take charge of the organization when their times comes. This is for both the board and management. In many organizations board members' supposed limitations of tenure are not observed. I have worked with organizations that have board members who have been sitting on the board for 30 years while their by-laws say a board member can only serve for a maximum of two consecutive years. No one should be indispensable because *When a reed dries up, another one grows in its place.*

Lastly, the central message of leadership, in spite of all the challenges, must be one of hope and not despair as it is hope that is the source of energy that drives change. The role of leadership must not be to hide nasty aspects of reality but rather to show that *Ants united can carry a dead elephant to their cave.*

Conclusion

In summary, *ubuntu* practice of leadership emphasizes that leadership is by its very essence participatory in nature, but it is important to separate the myths and realities of participatory leadership and decision making. This separation will add a lot value to the practical relevance of the concept of participatory leadership and decision making. Participation means different things to different people; no one leadership style is better than another; leaders tend to have natural tendencies that make them biased and therefore more effective in some styles than others. Decentralization will make participatory sense only if it moves beyond deconcentration. Finally, participatory leadership is not always good and autocratic leadership is not always bad.

Whatever form of participation a leader takes, key to its success will be the leader's interpersonal skills, values and attitude, though these are less emphasized in organizations where rationality and logic are emphasized. The leader needs strong skills in listening, empathy and creating a sense of presence. He or she also needs to be perceived to be transparent, honest, respectful and trustworthy. Leaders must be able to listen and must be able to respond to what is being said. The leader also needs courage to act and the ability to say no, even if this means displeasing the followers, as long as this is done in the spirit of dialogue and commitment to the shared vision and strategy. The two proverbs *If you want to arrive fast go alone and if you want to arrive far go with others* and *The person who waits may wait forever* together teach the concept of situational and optimum participatory leadership and decision making, guided by factors at play and the need to balance process and output.

Reflection Proverbs

What lessons can we learn on leadership and decision making in organizations from the following proverbs?

If you want to arrive fast go alone, if you want to arrive far go with others

If the sun says it is more powerful than the moon, then let it come and shine at night

The cat in his house has the teeth of a lion

When one reed dries up, another one grows in its place

There is more wisdom in listening than in talking

Ants united can carry a dead elephant to their cave

How can we use the lessons to improve leadership and decision making in our organization?

Board Performance Assessment Tool

Rate how your board is performing on each one of its functions below 0 = non-existent and 5 = excellent

Responsibility	Rate 0 - 5	How the organization is currently doing this	Improvement and suggestions
Being custodians of the organization			
Appointing and firing the director and senior staff			
Advising and supporting the director			
Managing conflicts			
Managing leadership successions for the board and management			
Reviewing and creating policies, systems and procedures			
Monitoring the organization's performance in relation to its mission and strategic plan			
Enhancing the organization's public image			
Ensuring legal and ethical integrity of the organization plus ensuring transparency and accountability			
Recruiting and orienting board members and assessing board performance			

Which functions is the board strong on? Which ones is it weak on? How can we build on the strengths and address the limitations?

Chapter 5

CULTIVATING MANAGEMENT EXCELLENCE

A person is taller than any mountain they have climbed

Introduction

In this chapter I will discuss the *ubuntu* principle of loyalty at individual level, in contrast to staff attraction and retention efforts discussed in the previous chapter. Loyalty means putting the organization and its interests first. It means being committed and dedicated to the mission and the cause of the organization. It also means supporting efforts aimed at fulfilling the mission of the organization and opposing those deemed to be aimed at derailing it from accomplishing its mission. This means that commitment to the mission of the organization supersedes all other loyalties. In short loyalty means taking one's work as an opportunity to serve rather than just merely as a means for survival or accumulation of wealth and power. Loyalty therefore requires the highest level of professionalism and commitment to both organizational development and self development. It involves understanding and commitment to the values of the organization.

Loyalty also means the ability to know when one has made one's contribution and outlived one's usefulness in the organization, and therefore gracefully bowing out to give room to others or allow new blood to make its contribution as well. It is important to note that loyalty also means being committed not only to the organization and its mission but also to the profession and what it stands for. In this chapter I will discuss the concept of loyalty by reflecting on my own personal and self development journey.

Showing Loyalty through Cultivating Excellence

The child that washes their hands will eat with kings

In most traditional African societies, at meal times, adults ate separately from the children. The adults usually had more and better food than the children. The children were deliberately given less food so that they could develop the fighting spirit through competition for the food. Eating from the same plate, they could fight and compete for the food and the stronger ones would get more food than the weak ones. Being a child therefore was not always pleasant, especially when it came to meal times. The adults on the other hand had more and better quality food as 'recognition' for their having survived and succeeded in their competition for food and therefore survival as children.

The adults however needed a small boy or girl to help them with the plates. Helping the adults with the plates had the privilege and advantage of access to more and better quality food than the rest of the children. This released one from the competition the rest of the children were subjected to. But to be identified and selected as one that would serve the adults one had to qualify. This privilege was given on merit. The adults looked for the child who 'washed his or her hands'. They looked for a child who was smart. They looked for a well-behaved child. They looked for a responsible child. They looked for the best among the children. Serving the adults was recognition for such characteristics.

This chapter will discuss how managers, especially young managers in non-profit organizations can 'wash their hands' so that they can achieve distinction and recognition in their work. 'Washing hands' means first and foremost being effective managers in serving the people the organization exists for and the people one is leading. Many times managers strive to please their seniors and donors. While these obviously need to be pleased, true success can only be determined by how well the organization achieves its mission or how well it serves the people it exists for.

The inspiration to write this chapter came from a reflection on the years I spent working as a programme manager for a community based agricultural development programme. I was resident in the community where the programme operated and during those years, I learned that weak project management is a major contributor to the failure of development projects and non-profit organizations in general. I also observed that a number of challenges hamper effective implementation of projects. Interaction with fellow professionals working in the same capacity in different organizations all over the world has provided further inspiration to share my experiences in this chapter. In this chapter I describe five lessons which proved to be very useful. While these lessons may reinforce the knowledge of more experienced managers, they will be especially appealing to those who are new and less experienced in the practice of non-profit management. By applying these lessons these managers will be able to 'wash their hands' and gain the distinction and recognition they need.

Lesson One: Get Focused

In a situation where funding is not easy and demands from the people the organization is serving are legion, it is a big challenge to be focused. Such situations force non-profit organizations to do 'anything as long as it brings money to the organization'. The organizations will 'stretch' their visions and missions to justify why they are picking some projects which 'do not quite fit'. This has negative implications for the managers who may be pushed in many directions.

Given such circumstances, the critical questions of 'what does the organization want to achieve?' and 'How will it be done?', though seemingly obvious, are usually not clearly answered by the managers. However, for the project to be successful, the managers must define clear answers to these questions in order to get focused. There are many possibilities and many tempting directions. The principle of focus is that *There are so many good things in life but they are not all meant for you.*

Success attracts so much attention that if not well handled may make the manager or leader lose focus. The proverb *Failure is an orphan but success has many relatives* illustrates this point well. The key lesson and caution to managers and leaders can be found in the saying *Beware of other people, other people have a lot of plans for you but those plans are usually not in your best interest.*

Self-confidence and self-knowledge on the part of the managers are important prerequisites for getting focused. 'Know thyself' is a valuable advice for managers. Self-knowledge provides the foundation for future development and stability of the individual managers. While self-assessment tools can be quite helpful, improving managerial skills and self-knowledge is a life-long process that has to be approached in a well planned manner, because *There are no short cuts to the top of a palm tree* and *The greatest investment one can make is to invest in oneself.* Focused managers can appreciate more and better the need for organizational focus. Such managers view organizational visions as an extension of their own personal visions. This link is important for organizational focus.

Self-development for Managers

The shadow as a block to leadership and management potential

The shadow refers to part of ourselves that we deny. According to Johnson quoted in Kaplan (1998: 5) the shadow is 'the part of ourselves we fail to see or know...the shadow is that which has not entered adequately into consciousness. It is the despised quarter of our being. It has an energy potential nearly as great as our ego.' If we fail to bring our shadows to consciousness we live unfocused and unintegrated lives, a fact we cannot stand. Our lives are characterized by contradictions which are too strong for us to deal with. As long as it is in the unconscious, the shadow despises our determination to change. While it is not possible to live perfect lives, a great deal of self-development is about turning as much of the shadow as possible into light. This is the essence of self-knowledge. Self-knowledge is therefore about dealing with one's shadow. It is about dealing with Plato's observation of the contradiction, The real tragedy of life is not children fearing the dark but adults fearing the light.

Means for self-development

According to Drucker (1990), leaders are neither born nor made; they are self-made. Self-development starts with identifying an ideal or higher cause outside oneself that one can serve. Organizations provide the task environment for the realization of one's ideal. Though they must be rewarded, true leaders and managers do not go out to amass wealth and things for themselves. The first principle of self-development is to establish one's purpose in life. When this is done all of the person's life revolves around that purpose. It becomes his focus and all consuming passion. Without this there can be no self-development. After one has established their ideal, they can now start asking themselves what it is going to take to achieve that purpose. This will help the individual to discover their strengths and weaknesses that they need to work on. It is only after this that one is ready to explore opportunities and needs in detail and match their internal capacity of competences and ability. Self-development must result in improvement of what one is already doing and changing to new things if need be.

Leadership development exercises

Exercise 1: Power paradigm shift

This exercise helps the leader to make a conscious power shift from a negative use of power (autocracy) to a positive use of power (empowering democratic orientation). Together participants explore the following questions:

1. How comfortable are you with your own power? What issues do you need to clear up in order to be more comfortable?

2. Who are your role models for the constructive use of power?

3. What did/do these role models give you that is helpful? What do you see in them that is not helpful?

4. For what aspects of power do you have no role models? What habits have you adopted in their absence? How well do these habits work for you?

5. What would it look like if you used your power with confidence and were comfortable with that power?

6. What fulfilling avenues for expressing power are not included in your current role? How important are they to you?

7. What is your ideal role and use of constructive power? What are the issues to be resolved for you to get to your ideal and what action points shall you take?

Exercise 2: Turning points

The aim of this exercise is to help an individual to understand themselves better by identifying patterns in their life that have a great bearing on their personality and leadership capacity. The exercise is done with a speaking partner.

Identify three major events in your life which resulted in significant changes in your life (try not to choose very emotional events as they blur objectivity):

- Describe clearly and in detail the event so that a word picture is formed between the two of you.

- Explain in detail how you handled the event or situation. What were the responses, rationalizations, emotions, actions etc.? The role of the speaking partner is to question, challenge and help you surface what you forgot or felt was not very important. He or she also helps you face what you are avoiding and what you are omitting.

- After the experience, what changed? Which of the changes were sustained? Did your attitude to certain things change? What was really different?

- Compare the three experiences and identify the patterns across the experiences. Based on these can you identify the same patterns in your life in general?

- What lessons then do you draw for yourself? What insights do you have now about the way you learn, handle change or develop? And what does this tell you about your leadership of self and others?

This exercise can be done in workshops but it works better when the level of trust is high. It therefore makes sense to have it towards the end of the workshop when relationships have developed.

Exercise 3: Dealing with personal immobility (exploring one's shadow)

When done regularly, this exercise helps one to continually bring the shadow into light. This is a more difficult exercise because the shadow will resist being exposed with all its might. It requires more commitment and determination.

- Identify an issue causing immobility in your life. This is an issue that despite all your effort you can't get quite over. This could be a relationship, an attitude or a general way of looking at the world. Usually this makes you blame anybody or anything but yourself.

- Choose a specific incident as a typical example of the issue.

- Reflect on it and describe the incident in clear detail and make it as real as possible, and try to relive it.

- Clearly describe what you did in the specific situation. Don't focus so much on what the other parties did but focus on what you did.

- Focus on the failure that resulted and ask yourself:

- Which part of me was involved in the situation?

- What did I lose through this incident?

- What did I gain? What part of me was winning or threatened? Was it a part that I am conscious of or not? What could it really be? My public image, personal pride etc? Resist blaming and face the shadow.

- Characterize your shadow which you have surfaced through this exercise. Describe it and put it before you and own it. If you reject it, it goes back to its safe place, the unconscious, and regains its power over you. When you master your shadow by making it conscious, you can transcend your previous limitations and more effectively and positively influence others, because your projection of them is the projection of your own liberation from your shadow. This is clearly illustrated in Christ's admonition, 'Remove first the plank in your eyes before you can remove the small stick in your friend's eyes'.

- Work with the exercise on separate incidents and expose a much as possible of your shadow, then work out an action plan on specific action points to break the chain of the shadow.

Exercise 4: Personal life management exercise

The way one uses his or her resources, time, money and emotional energy is a direct clue to one's true values and personality. By reflecting on these a person would know whether the values he or she practices are truly representative of who she or he wants to be, and therefore provide a basis for change.

A way of doing this would be to assess the percentages of time and emotional energy invested in various aspects of life. By anticipating how these might change over the years, the person may be able to change and modify his or her behaviour in order to prepare for the future – this is the essence of life management.

Life Area	% of time
• Physical health • Mental health • Spiritual health • Career development • Leisure • Marital relations • Parental relations • Filial relations • Social relations	
Total	100%

1. How are the percentages likely to change over the next five years?

2. What are the implications for the decisions I have to make today?

3. What behaviour and values should I then embrace?

When connected to one's vision, this exercise helps one to live a focused and balanced life. This exercise works better when one is aware of the typical characteristics of different stages of human development over the years of the lifespan.

Field based managers are usually the main link between the community they serve and the organization or the headquarters. Community expectations are usually far greater than the organization can deliver. Sometimes community pressure to expand project services can be quite high. The field managers need to keep clear limitations of organizational capacity. There is always a temptation to make unrealistic promises that will not be fulfilled, causing frustration to the people, and sooner or later leading to their loss of trust. Bill Cosby illustrates this point well when he says, *I do not know the key to success but the key to failure is trying to please everybody.* You have to disappoint a good number of people so that you can move forward. This is part of the sacrifice one has to make for self development and personal effectiveness.

Lesson 2: Be Courageous

Managers need to be bold and courageous leaders. There are many intimidating factors that will affect performance. Establishing one's position and authority may not be easy for new and young managers. The box below suggests ways in which managers can be more effective.

As seen in the previous chapter, there is a revolution today in the direction of participatory methodologies in management in which there is an element of power sharing in organizational settings and in decision-making processes. While this is far better than autocratic approaches, it should not be misunderstood to imply that the influence and authority of the manager should be diminished. Being participatory does not mean losing legitimate authority.

Improving one's effectiveness as a manager

There are a number of ways in which one can improve one's effectiveness as a manager. (i) Increasing and improving one's expertise – people usually respect people who have the expertise which they need for the job. A manager must make an effort to deepen and expand their expertise base to include the skills needed not only by subordinate colleagues but also by those more senior. (ii) Information capacity, which is related to expertise capacity – a manager should make sure that he or she is updated on current non-profit and development issues and other related news. People will always need this information and the manager should be able to provide it. (iii) Connection capacity, that is, having access to or relationships with influential people – the manager will increase his or her effectiveness through maintaining good relations with local leaders and other influential people in the community. It is the responsibility of the manager to make an effort to establish relationships of trust and respect with the local leaders. Attending or being part of social activities like funerals and weddings can help establish these relationships. However, a great deal of wisdom must be exercised in maintaining one's identity as a professional. 'Excessive rapport' must be avoided at all costs. (iv) One must always behave with integrity – it is very difficult to take a strong stand in a situation which you have contributed to the problem

Adapted from French and Bell, 1995, Raven (1959), Raven & Kruglanski (1975) and Natemeyer (1979)

A manager should make sure that his or her leadership and proper respect are intact all the time. It is also important to keep appropriate social distance with subordinates while at the same time being friendly, democratic and participatory. This will help the manager to be taken seriously and give him and her courage. One way of maintaining the right social distance is through a supervisory approach. A good reporting system which is easy to manage, such as weekly time sheets, will often prove to be quite successful. When the system is properly implemented and monitored, this reduces the need to police subordinates on a daily basis. It also takes away the perception that the manager is bullying his or her subordinates.

Many organizations have a culture of respecting adults which may impede effectiveness when a young manager finds himself or herself in charge of colleagues as old as his or her parents. In such instances, a situational approach to management can be very useful in reinforcing one's influence by dealing differently with each member of staff according to their experiences and capabilities. I remember an incident when two of my colleagues were in conflict. One was some years senior to my own mother and the other far younger. The one who was wrong was the older one. This put me in an awkward situation. I was torn between my professional ethics and cultural obligation – to respect the elderly. It took a great deal of courage to resolve the issue with wisdom and justice.

Managers working in field offices and communities know and understand ground realities better than senior staff and those at headquarters. They are responsible for giving accurate feedback to headquarters. Since the interests of the community and those of the organization may not always be congruent, courage is required in representing the community to the organization. In particular, it may not always be easy to suggest necessary modifications to the projects the organization is implementing, even though these are based on observations and feedback from the beneficiaries. Yet the knowledge that the project is serving the felt needs of the people is a great source of confidence.

For example, the original focus of the programme I worked for was agricultural development in an area situated eight kilometres from an expanding town, with another small but expanding township nearby. The programme had started 10 years previously, before the effects of the town had been felt. The programme originally targeted both men and women, yet in time most of the participants at the meetings and project activities were women because men had gone to work in town. In addition, it was becoming clear that agriculture was no longer the sole occupation of the people in the villages. Most of the women took advantage of the markets in town to start their own small businesses. They were now demanding that programme staff should help them with business skills and loans in addition to agriculture. Despite growing indifference from the community, the programme did not want to be derailed from its original focus. It could either continue as it was and become largely irrelevant to the needs of the people or recognize the reality of the local situation by appreciating the change in the people's livelihoods. It required a lot of courage on my part as a manager to convince staff at headquarters of the need for change.

Lesson 3: Learn from Other People's Skills and Experiences

While experience is a great teacher and its value cannot be over-emphasized, there is a great wealth of knowledge and insights to be gained from other professionals and practitioners – especially those who have been in the practice longer. Sharing challenges and successes with other professionals and practitioners can be quite relieving. Collaboration can complement one's skills and expertise. The multidisciplinary nature of non-profit and development work requires that the professional island mentality be shed, facilitating professional workers' move from independence to interdependence. For collaboration to be effective, each participant should have something to offer. It is a give and take deal. It is *quid pro quo*.

This also introduces the issue of collaborating with other development or non-profit organization workers who are focused on the same area. Non-profit projects are usually established to complement the work of government. Generally, either the government has pulled out altogether in that particular area, or the services provided are having little impact because the system of delivery is weak, through lack of both resources and motivation on the part of staff. This means that the non-profit manager must collaborate with the government staff working in the same area. Government staff are usually well equipped technically. This can be complementary to the manager's non-profit organization work. For instance, involving government extension development workers in our extension work significantly improved the quality of our work for the beneficiaries. Joint planning of activities with the government extension workers proved helpful in ensuring joint work and minimizing conflict. However, this may have its own problems, usually arising from differences in approach. The participatory approach promoted by most non-profits often clashes with the top-down culture in most government institutions. This difference may cause the beneficiaries to be confused, as they see the non-profit organization and government staff as being in competition. Joint planning and collaborative activities reduce this perception. Even government institutions are now moving from centralized to decentralized and more participatory approaches, and these types of relationships provide learning opportunities for their staff. While government staff benefit by learning about practical participatory approaches, non-profit organizations benefit from the technical expertise of the government staff.

Relationships among non-profit organizations have proved to be very useful in improving such organizations' effectiveness. Non-profit organizations doing similar or related work have a lot to share and learn from one another. Arranging inter-organizational visits and creating other useful relationships has proved a successful support mechanism for managers. Making use of non-profit consultancy expertise may be more appropriate than hiring commercial consultants who do not have non-profit expertise.

Many inter-organizational conflicts can be avoided by joining some associations or fora at district or regional level. Joining such bodies will enable the manager to learn about other organizations that exist in the area, what they do and how they can possibly work together. When I made a decision for our organization to join the district development committee (a committee that brought together all development actors, both governmental and non-profit), it opened our organization to wider recognition. While we benefited from the interaction, the other organizations also benefited from our organization, as we realized for the first time that we also had as much to share as we had to learn from the others.

Joining networks and professional groups can be of immense value. However, many networks have floundered because some members have only been on the receiving end and the others have felt that they were contributing more than they were benefiting. Groups will last only if there is a fair balance between what is given and what is received by its members. Managers should make a commitment to contribute to the success of such networks by contributing what is expected of them. The temptation to join too many professional associations at once should be resisted since this reduces one's ability to contribute; managers must be realistic about their commitments.

Another way of learning from other people's experience is to identify a coach or a mentor, especially for young managers. A critical issue in this decision is to make sure you identify the right person who can truly help because *Advice is like mushrooms, the wrong type can kill*. A mentor is someone who has succeeded in a professional field and is prepared to help less experienced persons to grow. I was fortunate to identify or rather be identified by an old retired professor who had been teaching African History in different universities for over fifty years. He helped me over a period of about five years to challenge myself and rethink what I thought I knew about development and organization development. Eventually he helped me to redefine these. The result was my conviction to undertake pioneering work in using proverbs as a tool for development and organization development. I am sure that without his mentorship and coaching this awakening may not have come to consciousness.

Lesson 4: Do not Lose Touch with the Ground

Project and programme managers are also normally responsible for administration work. Because field officers are normally responsible for making field visits and meeting beneficiaries, programme and project managers can easily become alienated from field work and field realities. Programme and project managers should not grow too tall to fail to stoop to the ground. They should make an effort to spend a fixed percentage of their time (not just a few minutes) in the communities working with both field staff and beneficiaries. The saying *Never be late twice* can be taken to mean that one can go to the community late but should not delay in making a second visit.

Strong local leadership is an important prerequisite for the success of development and non-profit efforts in the community. Although local leaders are usually preoccupied with community administration it is necessary to get them involved because their cooperation and blessing are indispensable for project success. Making an effort to learn the local language if this is necessary can be a great asset to the manager.

The paradox that exist in most non-profit organizations today is that the people who are put in the front line are those least equipped to do their work. Community situations are so complex that the people who are working directly with the beneficiaries are often the least experienced and rewarded. When they begin to demonstrate competence, they are usually promoted and taken away from where they are needed most. It follows that field staff are often the least motivated to do their work effectively. One of the main causes of the failure of development and other non-profit efforts is the lack of motivation, frustration and dissatisfaction of field workers. Unmotivated field workers cannot be expected to motivate the people with whom they are working; they cannot give away what they do not have. There is need for many non-profit organizations to review the incentives and rewards for field workers, yet this will not be fully appreciated if managers do not spend enough time in the communities to understand the reality of the field workers. People will achieve much more when they are motivated – when they are given challenging work which they also like. The proverb *Send a boy where he wants to go and you will see his best pace* emphasizes this.

One of the striking observations I made through spending time in communities was how difficult it is to encourage the poorest people of a community to participate in development work. Poverty is itself a big hindrance to participation in such activities. The poorest people are often unable to attend project meetings and activities since they are too busy looking for means of survival. Yet if deliberate efforts are made to target the poorest, the vested interests of the elite will be aroused. Elite members of the community may feel threatened by disempowerment, which may make them attempt to frustrate the development effort. A typical example occurs when targeted inputs such as subsidized fertilizers end up mostly in the hands of the better off rather than the poor for whom they are meant. The poor cannot be empowered by disempowering the better off. This makes it very difficult to work with the poor. Managers of participatory development projects face a major challenge here. Can the poorest members of the community really be successfully targeted for development work?

Another observation was the effect of past development failures on the present project efforts in some communities. Development practitioners and managers sometimes forget that they are often not the first to implement projects in the particular area. Comments like 'we tried that before and it did not work' are not uncommon. Such failures act as de-motivators for new efforts because usually people do not differentiate past and new approaches, as they all come in the name of development. However, the same failures can be taken as a starting point for clarifying the approach taken by the new project.

Lesson 5: Do not Lose the Learning Spirit

Development and non-profit work are dynamic fields. Unlike other fields, new insights are coming everyday, hence the need to be updated all the time. Access to modern communications like the internet can be a great professional advantage. Generally non-profit organizations do not optimize their use of information technologies. In many non-profit organizations, the computer is used only as a typewriter, the internet is used only for sending e-mails. There is low capacity to use these facilities as management tools.

Professional development should be a priority through whatever means are available. Registering on courses by correspondence can be a great help in putting learning into an organized framework. I started development work as a development facilitator with a bachelor's degree in 1996. After a few years I registered with a university for a master's course in development studies. I studied by distance learning and graduated three years later. I also studied for a doctorate by the same means and graduated four years later. Because of the new qualifications and demonstrated improvement in performance resulting from application of the studies I quickly moved to levels of more responsibility much faster than most of my colleagues. Time taken to read and reflect on experiences is a worthwhile investment for future effectiveness and efficiency.

Documentation is a powerful way of remembering what we have learnt and systematically building on our experiences. This is because *The palest ink is stronger than the strongest memory*. The culture in most non-profit organizations, like African culture, is oral in nature. Experiences, skills and knowledge are passed orally from person to person and from one generation to the next and subsequent ones. I remember sitting at an agricultural extension community meeting recently when an expatriate facilitator was explaining to community members how to make pesticides using indigenous plants. After she had finished, an elderly man stood up and said, 'All that the extensionist has said is true. In fact there is nothing new; this is what we were doing before the use of chemical inputs. In fact there is more that we know in addition to what she has said, but our problem is that we do not put our knowledge in books as she has done. Now these people have come to teach us what we should be teaching them.' The cultural weakness of not documenting our local knowledge and experiences has permeated even the professional arena. Many people are not keen to document what they have learnt. Writing has been left to researchers and academics who come to extract data and information for professional publications which may not have immediate relevance or practical use to our work as non-profit organizations working with people in the communities. By documenting our experiences we can make our contribution to the development process even greater as others will also learn from our experiences.

Conclusion

Young managers can 'wash their hands' by getting more focused, courageous, learning from other people's skills and experiences; maintaining touch with the ground and maintaining the learning spirit. This will enable them to distinguish themselves and gain the recognition they need in their organizations and in the field of practice. It is believed that when these elements are properly blended in the life of both young and more experienced non-profit managers, success becomes easier to achieve.

The main goal of this chapter has been to encourage managers to take time to reflect on the way they work in order to improve their effectiveness. The chapter has explored causes of success and failure in a particular context. It is hoped that the lessons learnt will be of relevance to managers in similar situations and that all other managers can at least get some insights. However, the lessons presented may not provide answers to all problems faced by non-profit managers. Depending on local context, both problems and solutions may be different.

Reflection proverbs

What lessons on self-development can we learn from the following proverbs?

A person is taller than any mountain they have climbed

The child that washes its hands will eat with kings

There are many good things in life but they are not all meant for you

There are no short cuts to the top of a palm tree

Advice is like mushrooms, the wrong type can kill

Send a boy where he wants to go and you will see his best pace

How can we use these lessons in supporting individual self development in our organization?

Management development assessment tool

Rate the following on a scale of 0 – 5 where 0 = non- existent 5 = excellent

Practice	Rate 0 – 5	Explanation
• The organization has an effective programme that supports individual self-development efforts		
• The individual managers are given challenging enough responsibilities and are allowed to innovate and make mistakes as long as they learn from those mistakes		
• The organization invests in 'networking' for the organization and individual managers as a way to improve managers' skills and competencies.		
• The organization makes it an official requirement that managers spend a certain agreed percentage of their time in the field to understand ground realities		
• The organization invests in the professional development of the managers		

Which practices is the organization strong on? Which ones is it weak on? How can we build on the strengths and address the limitations?

Chapter 6

CONFLICT MANAGEMENT IN ORGANIZATIONS

There is not a river that flows without a sound

Introduction

One day while driving in town with my daughter, who was nine years old at that time, I wanted to buy a music CD from a street vendor. I wanted a CD by Jimmy Cliff. She wanted a CD by a Zambian artist popular to girls of her age that time, K'Millian. There was enough money for only one CD. Since only one CD could be bought, who should get a CD became an issue. That was a conflict. Conflict can metaphorically be described as *Two people trying to sit on the same chair at the same time*. Who will get the resources when they are scarce, whose opinion shall we follow, whose approach shall we take, who will play what role and who determines that and whose values shall we adopt, are some of the common *chairs* where two or more people try to sit on at the same time, in organizations and in other situations in general.

Just as *There is not a river that flows without a sound* – that is to say, every home has its quarrels – conflict at manageable levels in organizations is normal and may even be an indicator of a healthy functioning organization. Conflict at manageable levels may also be necessary because *If two wise men agree on very point, then there is no need for one of them*. This means that conflict may help people see the same issue from different angles and hence to come up with better and sometimes complementary solutions. The existence of conflict shows that people are self-aware and that they know what they want. It is rumoured that the former president of Malawi Dr Hastings Kamuzu Banda asked the former president of Zambia Dr Kenneth Kaunda why the people of Zambia rioted so often while in Malawi people never rioted. Dr Kaunda replied that his people rioted because he was leading people who were alive. In this light conflict and its expression can be seen as positive things. They simply mean that people are alive and they know what is good for them and are willing to express themselves to get what they want. In families children are sometimes encouraged to 'fight' over small issues and find their own solutions as part of their self-development.

89

Conflict therefore is a neutral phenomenon. It becomes positive or negative depending on how it is managed. Positively, conflict can be used to bring justice where injustice and unfairness exist. In this way it can help provide an opportunity for new social and political systems in societies and organizations. When left to itself, however, or when badly managed, conflict may become violent and destructive, ultimately leading to loss of trust and breakdown of relationships. Conflict therefore becomes a concern only when it begins to have negative effects on the people and organizational performance. A recent major study in the UK revealed that nearly half of the human resource personnel responding to the survey manage conflict on a continuous basis in their organizations. They indicated that they spend an average of 160 hours per year dealing with conflict (Chartered Institute of Personnel and Development, 2008: 18). This indicates the magnitude of the problem of conflict the attention it deserves.

In this chapter, I will discuss reconciliation and joking relationships as the two key practices of managing conflicts in *ubuntu* cultures. Then I will go on to discuss the lessons modern organizations can learn for their conflict management efforts from these two practices.

Levels of Conflict in Organizations

Conflict in organizations may occur at three levels: intra-personal, inter-personal and inter-departmental.

At the intra-personal level, with rapid changes outside and within the organizations, individuals may fail to come to terms with the current realities and long for 'the old good days'. It is like the story of a professor I met in Madagascar who told me the world had become too complicated and he was failing to come to terms with all the changes and their implications and actually wished he was back in the 1970s when life was simple and less complicated for him. In cases of organizations that have shifted from informal stages to more formal stages of development, for example, individuals may not understand why they suddenly have to account for every expenditure they make, why they can no longer use the organization's vehicle for personal use and why they cannot simply walk into the director's office without an appointment. The newcomers may not understand why their qualifications are 'deliberately' not being recognized. They may not understand why their 'lack of experience' is such a big issue.

At the inter-personal level, conflict is normally between those who used to be powerful and those who are becoming powerful. It is about access to and use of power. For example, a clinical staff member may develop conflict with a new doctor. Similarly, there is often conflict between experience and qualifications. The veterans may be more experienced but have fewer qualifications while the reverse may be true for the newcomers. Preference given to one group may generate resentment from the other. As a result, these two groups may not work together well. Inter-personal conflict is often about access to and use of different sources of power in the organization.

At departmental level, conflict happens between different departments in the organization. The transition from a dependent phase to an independent phase in the organization, for example, may imply a change in priorities. This transition often implies more emphasis on the organization's field activities. Actually more and more donors are keen to fund activities and not administrative costs. While in the first phase the project departments and administrative departments might have been receiving the same attention, the shift to more emphasis on project staff may be a source of strained relationships between the project departments and administrative departments, for example.

Conflict may also happen at intra-organizational level. The whole organization may be in a conflict with itself often without fully knowing it. This often happens when there is a mismatch between what the organization does and what its task environment is asking of it. Changes in the environment may render the organization less relevant without the organization being conscious of it. This is often manifested through the organization's collective efforts and achievement not matching. There is often more effort as compared to achievement. It is also manifested through general frustration among the people in the organization. Unfortunately, people in the organization may spend their time pointing fingers of blame at each other without realizing that such a conflict is a call for the organization to do some introspection and re-examine its vision, mission and strategies.

Types of Conflict in Organizations

In order to effectively resolve, manage or transform organizational conflict, it is important to know the type of conflict one is dealing with. There are a number of ways to look at types of conflict. One way is presented in this section.

Conflict in the organization may take different forms. The form of the conflict is an indicator of how it can be resolved. Conflict may arise over resource use, facts, structure, or methods followed in doing work and values.

Conflicts arising out of scrutiny of the use of inadequate resources may result in strained relationships at all levels described above. Most conflicts in organizations are around competition for resources, particularly financial (though a friend of mine told me of a recent study indicating that the greatest source of conflict in US organizations today is people stealing other people's food from the kitchen refrigerator!). Tensions may arise because of financial crises and how to respond to them. Decisions to cut costs and make staff redundant are some of the causes of this type of conflict. This type of conflict is the easiest to resolve because it implies getting more resources. When the resources have been provided, the conflict will go away.

Another type of conflict is over facts, e.g. what results are we producing? Many non-profit organizations do not have effective monitoring and evaluation systems to objectively define their results. In this case people have different opinions on the results the organization is facing. When people argue over whether the direction is north or east the best way to resolve the conflict is to give them a compass. In a conflict over facts, therefore, the easiest way to resolve the conflict is to provide regular, objective information to the people concerned, such as financial and project narrative reports in easily accessible and readable form.

The structure of the organization may be another source of conflict. This is most often the case in situations where structures are formed before the strategic planning process or before the work of the organization has been adequately defined. People may fight for space. Others may do more work than they are supposed to while others do less. Others may be there who should not be there in the first place. The structure of the organization also shows people how they are supposed to relate to one another. When individuals are not comfortable in their positions, their relationships are negatively affected. Resolving this conflict involves redesigning and restructuring the organization to ensure that *form* follows *function*. The structure itself may also be a source of conflict. Many organizations have at least three structures at the same time. These are, first, the structure hanging on the wall or the official one; second, the structure that people would want; and third, the informal one in people's heads which they actually follow and use. When these three are not harmonized, they result in tension and conflict. This type of conflict is also related to policies, systems and procedures in the organization. Sometimes these are in conflict with what an organization is trying to achieve. I worked in an organization in a field office on a community based programme that needed staff to visit the communities every day, but the organizational policy required that all vehicles must be based at headquarters which was three hours away and that the managers had to apply for the vehicles, a process that took about three days to complete. The tension caused by this created a lot of conflict between the field and headquarters offices.

The fourth type of conflict is over work methods or approaches. Individuals with different methods or approaches may develop conflict over the right method for carrying out an assignment. While the organization should have a general approach to how it does its work, which provides a general framework for monitoring and evaluation, it must recognize that *There is always more that one way of skinning a cat.* Individuals, especially professionals, must be given the freedom to use their discretion. Results and not methods must measure them, as long as the methods fit within the general organizational approach and framework. Defining results, giving people all the support they need and then trusting them to use their knowledge, skills, experience and creativity is a way of managing this type of conflict.

The last type is conflict over values. Values are the deep-seated beliefs regarding what is right or wrong, what is important and not important. Values form individuals' mental models and ways of looking at the world. Most people believe that their way of looking at the world and things is right. We therefore tend to agree with those who look at the world and think like us and develop conflicts with those who do not. As they are systems of diversity, conflict is inevitable within organizations. There may be personal clashes because of personality differences, gender, different worldviews etc. The veterans may have different values from the newcomers. The newcomers may view the veterans as being conservative and having dictatorial tendencies, while the veterans may view the newcomers as not very serious or not understanding how much they suffered to get the organization where it is today. Sometimes there are tensions between staff and management as to the direction and strategy of the organization – often because of poor communication or the desire of individuals or small groups of staff to pursue their own agendas. This type of conflict may also arise because of the influence of some external stakeholder – maybe a donor, but more often a friend or a family member who seems to be pulling the strings from the background and appears to have excessive influence over key decision makers.

Conflict at values level is the most difficult to resolve, as witnessed globally through wars, divorces, divisions in political parties and churches, etc. The best way to resolve this type of conflict is to prevent it from happening. Once it reaches a critical stage conflict is almost impossible to reverse. Helping individuals to change mental attitudes and be able to appreciate things from another's point of view is to gain the capacity for empathy, a valuable skill for resolving conflict.

The above types of conflict may manifest themselves in different forms. Some of these are:

- Leadership and decision making – where should this organization be going?
- Role clarification – who should be doing what – who decides what I do?
- Power – who has more power – management or the board?
- Differing perceptions of the quality of what I do;
- People coming and taking away my turf;
- People giving me work beyond what I am paid to do;
- People not delivering on what I need them to do.

The Process and Stages of Conflict

Conflict is a process that goes through different stages. According to Tear Fund (2003: 12-13) these stages include:

Pre-conflict – this includes differences and tensions in the organization. Differences can be healthy and productive if met with tolerance. When tensions develop, views become fixed and people begin to criticize their opponents and view them as the enemy. Differences between the groups get worse. The groups become more divided. When differences develop into tensions there are unlikely to be any short cuts to an agreement.

Confrontation – This includes disputes. Neither side admits that it has made a mistake. They become determined and take more extreme positions, sometimes making threats that may not actually be carried out.

Crisis – This is the peak of a conflict, manifested through open hostility and violence. Communication between the groups stops. People become convinced that their views are in fact right. They mock, scorn and isolate the opponents. Threats are actually carried out. At this point violence erupts. Once the crisis point is reached there are no quick solutions. In organizations subtle force may be used as physical violence may not be as easy to administer.

Outcome – If unattended to force may run its course until one party wins or surrenders, a ceasefire is agreed or both parties are tired and exhausted. Outsiders may be called to intervene.

As seen from the types of conflict above, conflicts that may start simply as issues around access to inadequate resources may degenerate to the highest level of conflict, over values, which is represented as the crisis stage above. In dealing with conflict it is important to always handle it informally at first and only deal with it formally if the conflict begins to reach the confrontation and crisis stages.

The best time to treat conflict is in its earliest stages. It becomes increasingly difficult to treat conflict as it progresses through the different stages. A story is told of a hunter who picked a leopard cub from one of his hunting expeditions. He gave the cub to his children as a pet. The children liked the cub and developed a close bond of affection with it. However, with passing time, the cub was growing and so was its leopard or beast nature. The hunter and the children forgot that the cub was actually a leopard and that a leopard is a beast. On a number of occasions the cub threatened to attack the children but they all took it for a joke and just laughed about it. One day a small child went to a nearby bush and got scratched by some thorny shrubs. The cub, which was quite a sizeable leopard by this time, heard the cry of the child and as usual went to 'help'. The leopard licked the blood from the child's scratch. When the leopard tasted the blood, the full beast nature that had been developing all the time came alive. The leopard instantly became vicious and attacked and injured not only the children but the adults as well, before returning to the wild never to come back again. This story is where the proverb *Young leopards grow into big leopards and big leopards kill* comes from. A related proverb is *Great fires erupt from tiny sparks*.

Conflict Management in Organizations

Conflict is officially managed through the grievance and disciplinary procedures in an organization (Foot and Hook, 1999: 380). Conflict is however practically managed in different ways in most organizations.

According to Professor John Hailey (personal communication.) there are several possible ways.

The organization may ignore the conflict and hope that it will die out eventually. People hope circumstances will change or the particular board/staff members will leave. This is called a 'keep battling' approach. It is more like an approach parents may take when siblings keep continually fighting and they don't intervene, hoping that with passing time and more growth and wisdom they will stop their fights.

Leaders may take an autocratic approach and dictate how the conflict will be resolved, leaving the parties concerned with no word to say. This is called a 'leader solves all' approach. While this may be branded dictatorial, it may also show that the leaders are strong enough to point out who is right and who is wrong and they don't want to waste time when the situation is so obvious.

Leadership may organize a kind of day or event to try to surface issues and get the people to talk to surface issues and get people to talk to each other or just to be nice to each other. This is called the 'special event approach'.

Leadership may organize a series of training and cultural change events over a period of a year or more run by experienced and respected trainers and facilitators. This is referred to as the 'Organization Development (OD) disguised as training' approach.

Bringing in some sort of external facilitator or consultant to undertake a review, ask questions, surface issues and try to facilitate some kind of rapprochement or identify way forward is another way organizations use in addressing conflict. This is called the 'outsider solves all' approach. This may also involve using employee assistance programmes – a service that may also be used to mediate in conflicts.

Another approach is long-term OD accompaniment. This is where an external specialist with much experience and credibility works alongside the senior management team and the board to help them manage their way through current issues and tensions. This is called the 'high-level hand-holding' approach.

It is difficult to say which of the approaches is generally more effective than any other, as there is little hard evidence, especially in relation to non-profit organizations; but it is important to say all these approaches are of some value. Experience however shows that the first and last approaches are most likely to be effective in the long run – either the 'battling on' approach, which is the most common, or some kind of a long-term accompaniment. In practice such a long-term approach is very rare, expensive and exhausting for the consultant, the interim manager and all involved. In principle, however, this should be the most effective approach, especially for bigger and deep-rooted conflicts. The one-off interventions or events seem to be the least effective because they merely raise expectations and surface issues that may be left unresolved. This just creates further resentment and hassle.

The reality is that organizations need to use these different approaches at different times. They need to have a 'menu' or 'tool box' of interventions. The crucial thing is not so much which approach is used, but having the judgement to know when to use the right approach at the right time and having sufficiently skilled and credible people to implement it.

The key principle for helping parties in conflict is to maintain objectivity and neutrality. The proverb *You can not kill the rat when it is on your clay pot* means that conflict mediators cannot effectively help the parties in conflict when they are too close or have contributed to the conflict. For an organization, this means that leaders may be able to resolve some conflicts but not others. Knowing which is which takes maturity. It is far easier for leaders to intervene in conflicts over resources or facts and increasingly more difficult in conflicts over methods, structure and values. Everyone in the organization is involved in the latter, which makes it difficult to maintain objectivity. External support is usually needed.

Conflict Resolution and Transformation in *Ubuntu* Cultures

As the process of conflict progresses from the pre-conflict to the crisis stages 'wounds' and wrongs are inflicted and incurred. Social cohesion and harmony are disrupted. *Ubuntu* societies developed mechanisms aimed at healing the past wounds, restoring social cohesion and harmony and building a foundation for healthy future relations.

Principles of conflict management emphasized the values of trust, fairness and reconciliation. Conflict mediation and maintenance of relationships was a critical role of the king and the council. The difference between the *ubuntu* and conventional approaches to conflict resolution and reconciliation is demonstrated in the ways in which a Western mediator and an experienced African mediator may approach a conflict resolution situation. Brock-Utna (2001: 6) observed that the Western mediator may begin the exploration by retracing the steps of the parties to the starting point of the conflict, with the aim of getting to its root causes. But an African elder, considering the social realities, may start from a point further back and try to form a frame of social reference. He may ask such questions as: who are you and where are you from? Can you say something about your family? Where did you grow up? What do you do or what do you like doing? Answers to these questions may provide clues not only about immediate causes but also about longstanding grievances, and offer insight into the differences and similarities between the parties. It also forms an impression of the interests and needs, aspirations and motivations of the conflicting parties. By understanding these needs, interests, age and power differences the African elder is helped to get an understanding of the remote and immediate causes of the conflict.

The people were duty bound to attend court hearings and to ensure laws were upheld. As a result of this collective responsibility, everyone had a right to ask questions in an open court. The concept of openness was an important value, implicit in which was the belief that no one should be punished for anything correctly said in an open forum (Jackson, 2002: 8).

Conflict was managed systematically through a hierarchy of levels. Smaller conflicts were resolved at family or household levels and proceeded to higher levels through appeal if some parties were not satisfied with the outcome. At higher levels, different levels of representatives of the king were responsible. The gravity or seriousness of the conflict determined the level at which it would be dealt with. Only very big cases would therefore reach the king's or the queen's court. The goal of all conflict mediation was reconciliation and relationship building. Reconciliation has been defined by Kiniesberg (2001) as 'the process by which parties that have experienced an oppressive relationship or a destructive conflict with each other move to attain a relationship that they believe to be (minimally) acceptable'.

Generally the process would be led by the council of elders. Elders were respected as trustworthy mediators because of their accumulated experience and wisdom. Modern examples include Archbishop Desmond Tutu, former President Thabo Mbeki and Kofi Annan. The role of these mediators would mostly be pressuring the parties involved into helpful agreements, making recommendations, giving assessments, and conveying suggestions on behalf of the involved parties among others. They were expected to facilitate through listening, information clarification, promoting clear communication, interpreting standard points, summarizing discussions, and emphasizing relevant norms or rules in the process, helping the parties to 'see the big picture' and repeating the agreement already attained (Brocke-Utne, 2001: 11; Murithi, 2006: 32).

The Reconciliation Process

The actual process of conflict resolution and transformation involved five steps. These were:

Acknowledging responsibility or guilt – after listening to both sides of the story, and after some independent investigations by the council of elders, a judgment was passed on who was wrong. When this was done, the person who was wrong was encouraged by the council of elders and members of the community present to acknowledge wrongdoing or guilt.

After acknowledgement of guilt the next step was to move beyond confession to actual repentance and showing remorse. The guilty person was to show that they were genuinely sorry and would never repeat the wrongdoing. They were to demonstrate that they recognized and empathized with the wronged person over the pain their action had inflicted on them.

Beyond repentance and showing remorse the individual was expected to ask for forgiveness from the victim and the victim in return was encouraged to show mercy. It was believed that *He who forgives ends an argument.* After forgiveness was given, where possible and at the suggestion of the council of elders, the perpetrators would be asked to pay appropriate compensation or reparation for the wrong done. This was mostly symbolic, with the primary function of reinforcing the remorse of the perpetrators. It was usually meant to be payment in kind for the wrong done or damage caused.

The final stage was a ritual aimed at consolidating the whole reconciliation process. This was done by encouraging the parties to shake hands or share a meal at each other's homes, with the aim of building their relationships anew. Among the Acholi people of Uganda, for example, this involved the guilty being reconciled with the victim's family through sharing a bitter drink called *Mato Oput* – a bitter herb of the Oput tree. This symbolized the psychological bitterness that prevailed in the minds of the parties before the conflict was resolved, and also the closure of such a painful experience.

The rituals were also aimed at placing an obligation on the parties to stick to the agreement and to their commitment. The wider community also played a role by assisting with the implementation of the agreement between the parties. The entire community could check whether the parties were still committed in practice to their agreement. Communities were also expected to offer support if the parties needed face saving, empowerment and encouragement.

The above five steps describe the reconciliation process as practiced in *ubuntu* cultures. This process was used for dealing with common community problems such as family and marriage disputes, theft, damage to property, murder and wars. It was strongly believed that parties need to be reconciled in order to rebuild and maintain trust and social cohesion.

Joking Relationships

Another concept for managing conflict among the *ubuntu* cultures is joking relationships. Joking relationships are a way of preventing or managing conflicts or defusing tension. They involve individuals or groups combining friendliness and antagonism in certain social situations. In this case one individual or group is allowed to mock or ridicule without the other taking offence. This may be done purely for the fun of it and in the process to break the ice for freer talking in the case of an actual conflict. Joking relationships may exist between in-laws, between cousins and even among clans or tribes. I used to be very apprehensive every time my mother and father-in-law met. Their conversation tended to be hostile, antagonistic and sometimes bordering on tribalism. But what I noticed was that none of them took offence. It was only when I was told about the concept of joking relationships that I understood the nature of their relationship. I remember at a workshop in Madagascar how two participants, one from South Africa and the other from Madagascar, kept 'pulling each other's leg' or teasing each other throughout the workshop, sometimes to an extent that other participants felt was too much. But later we discovered that these two individuals had naturally bonded and formed a joking relationship. They actually became the closest friends in the whole group.

Joking relationships serve as a 'legitimate' space to use humour to speak the unspeakable and therefore break ice on otherwise very sensitive issues. Joking relationships take a preventive and maintenance approach to conflict management. They involve privileged disrespect and the only obligation is to take no offence from the mocking or provocation as long as the disrespect is kept within bounds of the custom. Joking relationships are privileged relationships because one is born into them or they are acquired through special relationships like marriage. For instance a man may be allowed to 'flirt' with the unmarried younger sisters of his wife by referring to them as his wives and sometimes even teasing them, but it is taboo to cross boundaries. Clans may mock each other, at funerals for example, in ways that may shock outsiders, but there are always expected limits to be observed. Black people calling each other 'niggers' is an example of a joking relationship. They can call each other 'niggers' without creating or taking offence but anyone outside the community calling them by the same name would create offence. On a trip to Zimbabwe some of the employees of the organization I was working with gave me a nickname which they use for mocking Malawians living in Zimbabwe or Zimbabweans of Malawian origin. But those employees were using that same term to illustrate that we had become friends and we could joke about serious matters. That was a form of a joking relationship. If somebody else called me by the same name I would take offence.

The use of humour in joking relationships removes tension and create space for dialogue if there are issues to be discussed. I present below my colleague Charles Banda's recollections (verbatim) of joking relationships as he was growing up in Zambia in the 1970s.

I cannot remember very well how this relationship was supposed to have started but given the hindsight I may recollect some of the things that I heard and saw in the 70s in Zambia. We were told that the Bembas of Northern Zambia and the Ngonis mainly from the Eastern Zambia assumed the relationship of cousins after the British colonized the then Northern Rhodesia. History records that the Ngonis defeated the Bembas and as a result of this there was enmity between the two peoples. However, with the passing of time and the coming of the British, the Ngonis started looking at the Bembas as their young cousins and started joking about their relationship. However, what has puzzled me over time is the fact when an event befalls any of these people, e.g. an incident that I remember is when a Ngoni man hanged himself within the compound, all the Bembas came out and were like mocking. That time we were young and could not understand why people were laughing and joking at the funeral. For example I recall seeing all the women that were mourning being chased away [by people] saying why would they be crying for somebody who had decided to kill himself. Similar incidents were repeated at the graveyard where it was very difficult to dig the grave.

Such joking incidents did not just occur at funerals but even at merry moments like weddings. Here too, the opposite a tribe would crack sort of disruptive jokes. What is important about the whole thing is that everyone took these incidents as jokes rather than potential conflicts. I do not know if this behaviour is what to day makes the Zambians call Malawians as 'our wives'. I know that this comes from football where historically they landed us (Malawians) a few defeats. But then in Zambia generally they refer to Malawians as Ngonis because we are in the Eastern Province – an extension of Chipata – and therefore they joke about it as 'our wives'.

Advantages of this:

In Zambia there are generally three big tribal lines; the Lozi/Tonga, the Bemba and Ngonis. The Lozis and Tongas have to some extent been aloof, being proud of their heritage, boasting of the Litunga and Kuomboka, come to think of it, it is now that they are showing a wider interest in the affairs of Zambia politically, otherwise their allegiance has always been with their local paramount chief, the Litunga. The joke relations have so far managed to bring sworn enemies to become good friends. I guess this is why in the Zambian elections it is usually not about tribal affiliations but rather individual capabilities!

When I was young and looking at these incidents [this custom] made funerals look very light and not the kind of solemnity that goes with it. This was the first time in my life when I saw what a person who had hanged himself looked like. The body was not removed for a very long time because they wanted a lot of people to see it and I guess to learn from the incident that if you do things like that people will come and laugh at you and leave your corpse hanging there for a long time.

The cousinship meant that potential tribal conflicts were minimized.

A proverb like *If a mad person slaps you and you slap him back then both of you are mad* would be used to downplay a seeming or genuine provocation to conflict with those whom one has joking relationships. By mocking the provoker that they are mad, and by their required obligation not to take offence, a conflict is averted.

Madden (1986: 197) reports how the concept of joking relationships was used among staff in an organization. A formalized joking relationship was established between senior and junior staff. Licensed humour between the two groups was employed as a device for both lending and asking for support. People could mock each other. This reduced tension. And this enabled them to raise serious issues in a light-hearted mood. Joking relationships helped reduce distance and helped created a more egalitarian environment between the two groups which used to have a more hierarchical relationship. Reduction of a hierarchical relationship and establishment of a more egalitarian relationship are key elements in managing conflicts in any group.

The essence of joking relationships is in building relationships to a depth that people know each other. This depth of knowledge is enough to prevent a lot of potential conflicts. Secondly, because there is a relationship of trust, when conflicts do arise they are easier to resolve as no party is suspicious of the other's motives. Conflicts get compounded when people or parties are unsure or suspicious of each other's motives. Joking relationships are aimed at cultivating friendship in the real sense of the word. Friends do not want to hurt each other. When something comes in the way, they can always talk about it or resolve it 'for old time's sake' or 'for friendship's sake'.

The reconciliation procedure of conflict resolution and reconciliation in *ubuntu* takes a curative approach to conflict, i.e. it deals with conflict after the conflict has already happened. The joking relationships procedure takes a preventive and maintenance approach. The joking relationships approach would therefore add more value to conflicts that have not reached the crisis stage, while the reconciliation approach would add more value to conflicts that have reached the crisis stage. Organizations need procedures for dealing with conflict before and after it has reached the crisis stage. These two approaches would add a lot of value to organizations in their conflict management efforts.

If Africa has such a potentially effective conflict resolution approach, one may want to ask, why is it that the continent has the highest number of conflicts in the world? If South Africa is seen as the leading proponent of *ubuntu* in general and this approach in particular, how can we explain the recent xenophobic attacks on fellow Africans for example? One of the answers to this is that *ubuntu* or this approach to conflict resolution and management has not really been given a chance. Western approaches have generally replaced this approach.

Ubuntu Conflict Resolution Lessons for Modern Organizations

The *ubuntu* reconciliation process does not belong only to the dead past. This process was used for example by the Truth and Reconciliation Commission in South Africa under the leadership of Archbishop

Desmond Tutu. Leaders from the commission and other organizations in South Africa have been invited to conflict hotspots in the world like Northern Ireland and Palestine to share their experiences and make a contribution on how this process can add value to the local conflict resolution and transformation processes. In Rwanda, the local courts or *Gacaca* courts employ a process to bring healing after the infamous genocide that killed about a million people in 1994. In Northern Uganda, local communities and the International Criminal Court are in dispute over how to end the war, with the ICC demanding that Joseph Kony and his colleagues should be handed over to the international justice system while the local communities see a reconciliation process (mentioned earlier) as a more realistically effective way to motivate the Lord's Resistance Army (LRA) to stop the war.

Key lessons that organizations can draw from *ubuntu* conflict management practices include:

- Acknowledging that conflict is part of organizational reality and putting in place mechanisms of dealing with it as a way of showing that indeed the organization accepts conflict as part of organizational reality.

- The need to invest more in preventive (joking relationship) type of measures, since in most organizations 'full blown' conflict is a rare phenomenon. I only know of one incident where a consultant was physically beaten by angry staff because they thought he had made recommendations to get them retrenched; police and an ambulance had to be called and the consultant spent some considerable time in hospital receiving treatment. But such incidents are rare. Prevention is better than cure. The regulatory framework for dispute resolution in the UK that came into force in 2009 provides greater encouragement and opportunities for managers to resolve disputes or conflicts informally before the formal disciplinary or grievance procedures come into play (Chartered Institute of Personnel and Development, 2008: 8).

- Organizations still need to put in place reconciliation mechanisms to deal with those conflicts that the informal mechanism may not be able to resolve.

- Organizations need to explore the concept of 'friendship' as used in joking relationships to improve relationships between individuals, groups, departments, and layers within the organization, and how this can be used as a means to prevent conflict. The concept of friendship in this context does not mean doing away with social distance that is required for normal functioning of business.

- The spirit of 'official' friendship as implied in joking relationships helps staff to resolve much of the conflict among themselves.

Managing conflicts should be taken as an opportunity for building capacity and a sense of responsibility among the staff. Lower levels of conflict must be dealt with at as low a level as possible. This helps to build trust among peers. Appeals should only be made if one feels dissatisfied by the solutions at the lower levels. Handling conflicts at the lower levels enables the people to be involved in the conflict management and hence in the relationship building of their organizations which is a key value in *ubuntu* cultures.

Conclusion

The *ubuntu* practices of joking relationships and reconciliation would add value to the common conflict management procedures in organizations, which include the 'keep battling', 'leader solves all', 'special event', 'OD disguised as training', 'outsider solves all', and 'high-level, hand-holding' approaches. Joking relationships would enable organizations to take a preventive and humorous approach to conflict management. Reconciliation would help organizations to mend the broken relationships and to rectify wrongs and restore justice. While the principles underlying the concepts of reconciliation and joking relationships may be universal, their application in different contexts may need adaptation to suit the different situations. It is also important to note that if not well understood and if wrongly applied both joking relationships and reconciliation can do more harm than good; and lastly, that joking relationships are for some people and not for all, and not all people in an organization can be comfortable with this type of relationship.

If the common metaphor for understanding conflict is *Two people trying to sit on the same chair at the same time,* it follows that the way to resolve conflict will be seen as one person or group winning with the other losing. Changing the understanding of conflict from *Two people trying to sit on the same chair at the same time* to *Two people or groups unconsciously trying to find common ground* changes the issues in conflict management to how we can increase resources to satisfy all (rather than who gets the scarce resources), what are the facts on which we can base our opinions (rather than whose opinion shall we follow), what is the efficiency or the cost effectiveness of the proposed approaches (rather than whose approach we shall follow), what are our strengths and weaknesses and where can we make the most contribution (rather than who should be doing what and who determines that), and finally can we agree to disagree amicably ? (rather than whose values should we adopt).

The shift from *Two people trying to sit on the same chair at the same time* to *Two people unconsciously trying to find common ground* would be a move from most conflict resolution practices in organizations today to what the *ubuntu* practice would represent; or it can be seen as a contribution that joking relationships and reconciliation would bring to the current conflict management practices.

Reflection Proverbs

What lessons on conflict management in organizations can we learn from the following proverbs?

There is not a river that flows without a sound

If two wise men agree on every point then there is no need for one of them

Young leopards grow into big ones and big leopards kill

If a mad person slaps you and you slap him back them both of you are mad

How can we use the lessons to improve conflict management efforts in our organization?

Reflection Exercise

What type of conflicts have we observed or experienced in our organization?

How are these conflicts resolved?

How can we make use of the principles behind the concept of joking relationships in our conflict management efforts?

How closely do our conflict management procedures follow the *ubuntu* reconciliation procedure of: acknowledging responsibility and guilt, showing remorse, repentance, asking for and receiving forgiveness, and finally a ritual for restoring broken relationship and trust building?

How can we use the concept of joking relationships to address conflicts in our organizations?

Chapter 7

KNOWLEDGE MANAGEMENT

It is not money that builds a house but wisdom

Introduction

The proverb *It is not money that builds a house but wisdom* teaches that money without wisdom is often wasted. Two individuals earning the same amount of money and with similar responsibilities may achieve differently depending on their values, priorities and wisdom. The proverb encourages individuals to seek wisdom more than money. Similarly it encourages organizations to seek wisdom more than they seek financial resources. Wisdom refers to how organizations manage their collective knowledge.

Every organization has three and only three resources. These are money, time and knowledge. Today there is more emphasis on money of financial management, some emphasis on time management (this is not entirely true especially in Africa) and relatively little emphasis on knowledge management. Of the three resources however, it is being recognized that knowledge and its use are the most important resources organizations may have. Knowledge management is being recognized as a key issue that organizations can no longer afford to ignore. The importance of knowledge management is emphasized by Thomas Stewart when he says, '*Growing around us is a new information age whose fundamental source of wealth are knowledge and its communication rather than natural resources and physical labour. Managing information, finding and growing intellectual capital, storing it, selling it, sharing it has become the most important task of individuals, organizations and nations.*'

Ubuntu cultures placed high priority on knowledge management. The proverbs *It is easy to defeat a people who cannot kindle a fire for themselves* and *Knowledge is like a baobab tree, no one person can embrace it alone* illustrate the high priority *ubuntu* cultures placed on knowledge management.

Traditionally, in African societies the elders would occasionally sit around the fire in the evenings to discuss issues of concern to the community in order to maintain stability and unity. If the fire is not kindled, for this purpose literally or symbolically, the proverb warns that the people will easily be defeated in the time of trial. One of the key roles of grandparents was to tell fireside stories in the evenings to their grandchildren. This was a form of entertainment but more important, it was a form of education in morals and character. It was a way of imparting values to the children. Children who missed this kind of education did not have a strong foundation and would easily be defeated by the challenges of life along their ways. Through these practices knowledge was created, stored, used and passed on to the next generations. The proverb means that organizations must *light a fire* or they will be defeated from within or outside.

I remember the night I was married. After planning with my wife that we would spend that night at some hotel in town for the honeymoon, we were told that this was not culturally possible. I remember the elders from both my wife's side and my side sitting around the fire talking with us as newly weds late into the night about marriage and family values. Almost fifteen years later, I believe this formed a strong foundation for my marriage and family.

A baobab is too big a tree for one person to embrace alone. The proverb *Knowledge is like a baobab tree, no one person can embrace it alone* therefore means that everyone's knowledge counts. We normally think people at the top know or that only a few people have useful knowledge but everyone's knowledge must be sought, respected and utilized.

The two proverbs together mean that organizations must set up systems that will help them decipher what is in people's heads, put it on the table, create common understanding of what the organization is and what it should be, and keep talking on how to get there.

The Meaning of Knowledge Management

Knowledge management refers to a conscious and integrated approach to identifying, creating, managing, sharing and making full use of all information and knowledge assets of an organization. Knowledge management is intended to improve an organization's innovation, responsiveness and adaptability (Levinson, 2008: 1). In short, knowledge management means making decisions towards innovation, responsiveness and adaptability are based on information and facts and not guesswork.

All the people in an organization have useful knowledge that can help the organization improve its innovation, responsiveness, adaptability and therefore impact. The key challenge however is to identify the different types of information and knowledge the people have and then put in place systems and practices to create a collective knowledge base out of individuals' information and knowledge, and store and manage that knowledge and share it or make it accessible to all in the organization as an asset for improving innovation, responsiveness, adaptability and therefore impact. Much of this knowledge remains in individuals' heads and there are no systems to make it available to all the people in the organization who may need it. The proverb *The death of an old person is like an entire library burnt* illustrates this point well. It says that old people usually have a lot of practical information, knowledge and wisdom that can be used to enrich life in general but usually there are no systems or ways to get this information, knowledge and wisdom from their heads and make it available to people in general. When these people die, they die with all the information, knowledge and wisdom in their heads and the world is left poorer. The proverb teaches that society and organizations must find ways to get the wisdom of the old people and old employees to society and entire organizations respectively. In this way society and organizations will be much richer. The information, knowledge and wisdom will be transferred from being individual to societal and organizational property and therefore these will be more accessible and useful. Knowledge management means creating an organization's knowledge bank and continuously investing in the bank while at the same time making maximum use of the knowledge for impact.

Knowledge Management in *Ubuntu* Cultures

Knowledge management is closely related to the concept of learning and organizational learning because an organization's knowledge base is mostly derived from its conscious learning practices. The insights from reflection on the organization's practice, for example, form a major part of the organization's knowledge base. In this section, I will discuss the learning process in *ubuntu* cultures and try to tie it up with knowledge management.

Professor Michongwe (2005 personal communication) defined African education as *the ability to use what one has collected through a learning process to develop oneself and one's community or country.* He noted that modern education, including most leadership development initiatives, emphasizes developing oneself and not one's community or country. If leadership development is to be effective, it must aim at developing individuals and their organizations. Many such programmes,

111

packaged as leadership training courses, are rarely transferred effectively from the individual to the organization.

Indigenous educational systems in pre-colonial Africa were aimed at passing on to the young the accumulated knowledge to enable them to play adult roles and so ensure the survival of their offspring and the continuity of the community. The older generation passed on to the young the knowledge, the skills, the mode of behaviour and the beliefs they should have for playing their social roles in adult life. They believed that *A child who does not cultivate relationships with the elderly is like a tree without roots.* The young were taught how to cope with their environment, how to farm or hunt, fish or prepare food, build a hut or run a home. They were taught the language and manners, and generally the culture of the community. Methods used were informal, with the young learning by participating in activities alongside their elders, as well as by listening, watching and doing.

The people recognized that the ways the young would fulfil their social roles would depend on the sort of persons they became. So they were taught the community's standards of conduct based on their shared values. Above all, they were taught that their behaviour was a matter of concern for all their kinsfolk, for whom the way they behaved and what they did would bring honour or dishonour. In different ways and situations, the young learned what the community regarded as good and what it regarded as evil, and caught the community's concept of the good life. This was training in citizenship. The greatest concern was shown about the sort of persons the young would become, and the life they would lead as members of the community.

The culture emphasized as the *summum bonum* a social sensitivity which made one lose oneself in the group: the kinsfolk were, and lived as, members of one another. It was the goal of education to inculcate this sense of belonging. The solidarity of the small, homogeneous group of kinsfolk; the close knit organization of the village, kingdom or tribe; the rituals by which their sense of belonging was constantly renewed; all of these were reinforced. Indigenous education sought to produce men and women who were not self-centred; who put the interest of the group above their personal interest; who dutifully fulfilled obligations hallowed and approved by tradition out of reverence for their ancestors, gods and the unknown universe of spirits and forces. There was always the awareness that human life was the greatest value, and an increase in the number and quality of the members of the community the greatest blessing the gods could confer on the living. Proverbs like *Even a madman has relatives; you will see them when he dies* illustrate this point well. Indigenous education also drew strongly on the spiritual dimension, which pervaded all activities and all relationships. Education inculcated a religious attitude to life, manifested in reverence towards nature and the unknown universe.

The indigenous education system used a variety of methods including work and play and religious rites; song and dance and folklore and proverbs; and customary services received or given within the all-embracing network of family and kinship ties.

The practical approach to education emphasized the importance of experiential learning or learning by doing as a way of dealing with new problems. They believed that *A person is taller than any mountain they have climbed* and that *A bird that has flown over a sea cannot be afraid of a river.*

Knowledge Management Lessons from *Ubuntu* Cultures

Seven lessons can be drawn from the learning and knowledge management practices of *ubuntu* cultures. These include:

Organizations must seek and create only knowledge that is critical to their success. Today the volume of information that organizations need to process on a daily basis is increasing at an exponential rate. Identifying critical information that the organization requires and ways to access, store and use it is an increasingly required valuable skill. The proverb *There are so many good things in life but they are not all meant for you* emphasizes this point well. There is too much information available but not all of it is crucial to the success of an organization. In addition, as competition for funding intensifies, organizations are expected to do more work with fewer resources. Knowledge is the lever that enables efficiency and effectiveness.

The knowledge that staff are seeking should always be linked to the needs of the organization. The first criterion in supporting individuals and groups seeking knowledge-enhancing opportunities should be how their knowledge will contribute to the organization's mission. In addition, before the people are supported, the organization should make sure that systems and practices are in place that will enable it to take the knowledge from the individuals when they come back. I remember sitting on an interview panel of a big non-profit organization where one of the candidates who was working for the government said she wanted to quit her job because the organization had sent her overseas to study for a master's course; she had been very excited about the course and while on it she had formulated many ideas she thought would help the organization when she came back; but when she did, no one wanted to listen to her because there were simply no systems to capture and make use of her ideas.

Knowledge management is primarily meant for the internal stakeholders of the organization – the staff, volunteers and the board. Many organizations make the mistake of thinking that knowledge management is about disseminating their lessons to their stakeholders. Being primarily focused on internal stakeholders, knowledge management must balance the three elements of the organizations – being, doing, and relating. It must be about getting information and knowledge that will help the organization improve, or about knowledge that helps the organization become what it wants to be in these three areas. The organization needs more conscious effort on knowledge that helps cultivate its being and relationships, as the natural tendency is to concentrate on the doing.

Knowledge must be practical in nature. This is why it is important to emphasize that the most useful knowledge is often obtained from reflection on the organization's own practice. Theoretical information and knowledge need to be tested before being accepted as the organization's own knowledge. Related to this, knowledge must be contextually relevant. The knowledge that an organization needs in Canada may in principle be the same as the knowledge an organization needs in India but in practice they may be different, hence the need for contextualization. This is why the most important knowledge that an organization must have is that which is derived from its own reflection on its practice.

The need for contextualization is illustrated by the story of an American professor who asked children at a primary school in Africa a simple arithmetic question: 'If there are ten sheep on one side of the road and one of them crosses to the other side, how many sheep will remain?' The children in unison all said that the answer was zero. The professor was confused because usually to him this was a very simple arithmetic question and the whole class wouldn't miss it just like that. When he asked why they said the answer was zero, the children said that from their experience and indeed the experience of anyone who has raised sheep, sheep follow what they called *'flock instinct'*. When one of them crosses the road they all follow and therefore none will be remaining on the other side of the road. In this story, it shows that in the context of the professor the right answer is nine; in the context of the children, the right answer was zero. Both of them were right according to their contexts. The moral is that one should not transfer knowledge from one context to the other wholesale without first contextualizing it. Organizations can and must learn from the knowledge and best practices from other places but make sure these are contextualized to ensure their usefulness.

Organizational knowledge must be accessible to all. Different people have different orientations as far as information or knowledge and its use are concerned. This is why the indigenous education system used a variety of methods including work, play and religious rites. The organization's knowledge management systems must demonstrate this diversity to ensure that all the people in the organization are accommodated.

Knowledge management goes beyond what people in the organization and therefore the organization know. Knowledge management includes who the people know and the positive relationships (those that make a contribution to the organization) they have with those people. When key staff leave, if there was no connection between their relationships or contacts and the organization they will often leave with these contacts and relationships, leaving the organization poorer. The statement *It's not what you know but who you know that matters* is very true, especially in organizations' knowledge management efforts. In Zimbabwe, at the time of writing this book, the economy had completely collapsed. I went to a hotel on a Friday and stayed there for a week. On the first day I bought my dinner at 400,000.00 Zimbabwean dollars (Z$); by Thursday the next week I bought the same meal at Z$ $ 2,000,000.00, even though getting access to cash was restricted. People could only get Z$ 20,000.00 per day, which could be enough only for getting a bus to and from one's office. Commodities were expensive but also extremely scarce. One wonders how people survive in such situations. A key survival strategy I was made to understand was *social networking* – forming networks of friends and relatives to support each other with survival and coping mechanisms, such as notifying each other where to find what commodities, lending each other cash, and sending some members across the border to buy some necessities for the network members. This is knowledge management in practice.

Knowledge management goes beyond just information and knowledge and their management. It also involves coming up with or identifying ideas that can cause the organization to leapfrog to success. If the organization cannot come up with such breakthrough ideas, it must develop capacity to identify and acquire these ideas from elsewhere. Research shows that a society's capacity to quickly and broadly adopt and adapt the innovations developed by others is at least as important economically as its capacity to come up with breakthroughs itself (Shapiro, 2008: 18). The same can also be said about organizations. Ideas can be a source of wealth and sustainability for the organization. Organizations therefore need systems to help them identify and then make full use of ideas. This is also where networks of organizations become an important factor in knowledge management efforts. Networks have the potential to provide a wider pool of ideas that individual organizations can access. They also provide opportunities for making use of ideas. An example is an organization in Zimbabwe that make a lot of money by going into partnership with a private company to produce medicinal products for export from a plant that was largely growing locally as a weed. Using this idea, the private company, the non-profit organization and the communities all benefited.

Of course a key shadow with African knowledge management systems is their oral tradition. Knowledge was passed from one group to the other and from generation to generation orally. Oral knowledge management has its strengths but it also has some serious weaknesses. The Indian proverb *The palest ink is stronger than the strongest memory* illustrates this well. What is committed to memory can be forgotten no matter how efficient that memory is. In addition, memory is limited in that it can only be accessed by the person in whose brain the information is. When that person leaves all the information leaves with him or her. In one organization, a group of old people fought threats of retrenchment because they had specialized knowledge. The organization was a water supply organization or a water board. These people happened to be among the first employees of the organization and they knew the city's water pipes configuration. Unfortunately the organization did not have the water configuration designs in writing. These people were immensely powerful because they were the only people who knew the configuration and therefore the only ones who could help with faults to do with the water system. The organization could only retrench them at its own peril. This put the organization in an awkward situation because relying on these people was not sustainable in the long term, as they would eventually and inevitably leave at one point or another. What a difference it would have made if the organization had the water configuration design in writing, no matter how dusty or pale the design documents, as indeed they were supposed to have done. The organization would be in a much better situation.

The proverb *The strongest memory is weaker than the palest ink* points out to the importance of adopting a documentation culture in knowledge management. There are generally high levels of staff turnover in non-profit organizations. Without proper knowledge management systems, when staff leave they depart with all their knowledge, experience and expertise. Knowledge management aims at creating 'organizational memory'.

Knowledge management is generally a new area in most non-profit organizations and therefore there is need for more awareness, time, money and organizational energy to be allocated to it. For this reason, I will take some time to briefly discuss what the process of knowledge management may look like in practice.

The Practice of Knowledge Management

The practice of knowledge management integrates five organizational areas: the knowledge management process, leadership, culture, technology and measurement. To ensure success there is need for specific responsibility to be assigned to the knowledge management initiative, which needs a champion and collective leadership.

The knowledge management process

This involves identifying knowledge gaps and following well-defined processes to close them. Both explicit knowledge gaps (what employees know how to do and can and do express, also including the organization's documented knowledge) and tacit ones (what employees know how to do and cannot or do not express) must be addressed. Tacit knowledge must be given as much value as explicit knowledge. The organization must put in place conscious knowledge gathering mechanisms. The process must be inclusive with all members of the organization involved in looking for ideas (in traditional and non-traditional places) to improve its performance. This is because *Knowledge is like a baobab tree, no one person can embrace it alone.*

The organization must formalize the process of transferring best practices, including documentation and lessons learnt. It must move beyond documenting best practices and lessons learnt, to putting in place a conscious system to ensure that the new knowledge gathered is actually integrated into practice.

Leadership in knowledge management

A crab's daughters cannot walk differently from their mother. A crab walks sideways and forward. No matter how much the mother crab may want her daughters to walk straight and forward the daughters cannot because they learn how to walk from the mother. The proverb teaches that the leadership of the organization must lead by example. It teaches that the leadership sets the tone on the value that the rest of the organization will put on knowledge management. The two areas leadership sets the tone are strategic planning and management; and organizational learning. Leadership must lead by example by walking its talk.

Managing organizational knowledge is central to the organization's strategic plan. In other words knowledge management forms a key part of the strategic plan and it must be consciously mainstreamed into all the components of the strategic plan. The critical role of knowledge management must be conspicuously visible in the organization's financial and organizational sustainability plans. The organization must consciously develop plans or strategies for identifying, storing, using, marketing and selling its knowledge assets. This among other things might mean consciously using its knowledge assets in preparing proposals and other marketing efforts or actually developing intellectual capital that can be sold for money.

The leadership must support and promote organizational learning to strengthen existing core competences and create new ones. Organizational learning refers to the changes in organizational behaviour that occur through collective learning processes in the organization. This involves learning from the failures and successes of the organization. It involves reflecting on such questions as: out of what we implemented, what worked well and what did not? What lessons or insights are we getting from the answers to these questions? How can we use these lessons and insights for more effective and efficient implementation? Organizational learning results in new insights or lessons from reflection on practice. The new insights when applied become core competences. Through the systems for hiring, appraisal and compensation or remuneration, leadership pays special attention to individuals' actual and potential contribution to the organization's knowledge and its management.

Knowledge management culture

A knowledge management culture is about creating an empowering and supportive environment to facilitate the practice of knowledge management in the organization. Creating facilitative space for knowledge management includes:

- A management which practices what it preaches, allocating time to effective creation, storage, retrieval and use of knowledge and actually enjoying it;

- An effective knowledge management system that is fed from processed primary data;

- A designated fund which staff can draw on for specific learning and knowledge management activities;

- Team building finance to bring together different perspectives on the same issues, project, relationships, or evaluations;

- Mandatory post-mortems on all projects closed in a particular period;

- Planned thematic studies to be carried out each year; and

- Annual review of projects on selected organizational objectives.

In summary, the organization encourages and facilitates knowledge sharing and a climate of openness and trust. Creating value for beneficiaries is acknowledged as a main objective of the organization's knowledge management efforts. There is flexibility and a desire to innovate and people are allowed to make mistakes in the process as long as they learn from the mistakes. Most important, employees take responsibility for their own learning rather than waiting for the organization to take lead in all learning opportunities.

The Content and Process of Organizational Reflection and Learning in Capacity Building Organisation (cbo)

Capacity Building Organisation (CBO) is a capacity building service organization comprising 10 professionals based in Cape Town but working throughout Southern Africa. CBO assists in the organizational change and capacity building of development organizations, a process which usually involves a series of engagements often spanning several months.

To improve the quality of their work with development organizations, CBO staff members are called upon to participate in a monthly reflection which lasts one day. In addition, a process of practice guidance ties together staff to share critical dialogue. The monthly review normally contains:

- A round up summary of work each professional is doing with the client organization to bring others up to date;

- Presentation of a case study in progress to highlight key features;

- Cross-organizational comparisons which draw out similarities and difference in organizational problems, and accordingly change strategies being considered or adopted;

- Reflection on the state of development organizations in the region and the forces they are dealing with;

- Testing of CBO's work profile against its own strategies and goals.

- Distillations of experiences are shared through CBO's annual reports, as well as contributions to journals and other publications. CBO is currently acknowledged to be a leading resource for not just doing but understanding organizational change in the region.

Three preconditions enable CBO to put reflection and learning into practice. First is the stance of the leadership which believes in action-reflection learning as a key to organizational effectiveness and contribution to development. This also provides the self-discipline necessary to ensure that staff are in Cape Town on the dates scheduled. Second is the type of financial support that CBO receives. In addition to charging, at a subsidized rate, for its services, CBO receives programme funding, not project by project funding. This has permitted long-term scheduling of reviews so that they have now simply become part and parcel of what CBO is. Third is the commitment to be a thinking as well as a direct professional resource to the development community; this is a specific organizational goal, also reached through a publications centre. *Adapted from Alan Fowler, 1997.*

Knowledge management technology

Technology plays a key role in knowledge management. Key functions of technology in knowledge management include:

- Linking all staff members to one another and to all relevant stakeholders;

- Creating an institutional memory that is accessible to the whole organization and over time, with new people who join the organization building on the foundation left by those who went before them;

- Bringing the organization close to the beneficiaries through fostering the development of 'client-centred' information technology;

- Supporting intra-organizational collaboration – this enables individuals and organizations to work together more effectively and reduce duplication.

Knowledge management measurement

Non-profit organizations' performance is measured on different levels including efficiency, effectiveness, impact, legacy and transformation (Malunga, 2007).

Efficiency refers to how well the organization is utilizing its resources of time, money and 'organizational energy' or skills and competences. Efficient use of resources is based on the organization's daily activities and must be measured on a monthly basis.

Effectiveness refers to how well the organization is implementing its strategies and how relevant those strategies are. Effectiveness must be measured on an annual basis.

Impact refers to the lasting changes happening in the organization's clients' lives as a result of its work. Impact is measured on a cycle of three to five years.

Legacy refers to how the organization wishes to be remembered – what mark it wants to leave in history. Legacy is based on the organization's mission and values. Legacy must be assessed on a 10-year cycle.

Transformation refers to the lasting, irreversible societal change that the organization has consciously helped to bring about. Transformation is change beyond recognition. It is of the magnitude of a caterpillar changing into a butterfly. Transformation is irreversible. Transformation is based on the organization's vision, and is assessed on a 25-year cycle.

An example of efficiency, effectiveness and impact would be a chicken rearing project with the aim of improving the nutritional status of children. The chicks, the feed and time given to raising the chicks would be a measure of efficiency, the eggs produced and the income from the sale of the eggs and the chickens would measure effectiveness. Reduction in malnutrition and the improved health of the children would measure impact. The children, after growing up and remembering how the project helped them when they were young, being inspired by this to help other children in similar situations would indicate legacy. And lastly, the project inspiring more similar projects, and the scaling up reaching a national scale with the possibility to cause a national shift in children's health, would indicate transformation.

It is the responsibility of leadership to create knowledge measures on transformation and legacy. It is the responsibility of management to create knowledge measures on impact and effectiveness. It is the responsibility of 'operations' to create knowledge measures on efficiency.

Finally, it is the responsibility of leadership to ensure alignment among all the levels of performance: efficiency, effectiveness, impact and transformation. The organization must develop specific indicators to manage knowledge at all these levels. The indicators on knowledge management must balance hard and soft as well as financial and non-financial measures. The organization should allocate resources towards efforts that consciously and measurably increase its knowledge base.

A Case Study on Knowledge Management

Knowledge Management in Youth Help

Background

Youth Help is an NGO that provides social services for children and youths. It has 800 staff members and five field offices. Youth help focuses on:

- Health development of children and youths

- Nurturing children and youths to be responsible citizens

- Promoting rights of youths and children

Between 2000 and 2004 Youth Help went through a Knowledge Management (KM) programme. Two reasons led to the need for the KM programme. These were:

High staff turnover due to problems with job security, better job offers in other organizations, poor conditions of service etc. When staff left, they left with their knowledge and experience, which led to poor organizational memory.

Practical needs - Youth Help observed that the challenges they were addressing were getting more complex, which meant that more and better knowledge was needed to address them.

Implementation of the KM programme

In 2000 Youth Help's senior management started exploring the concept of KM. They referred to many books and articles. They hired some consultants for a KM awareness workshop. At the end of the workshop, Youth Help selected a KM project management team and some pilot teams to implement the Km programme. In order to change organizational culture and promote the KM programme, some staff member briefing sessions were provided.

In 2003, a KM platform was designed and installed. It was a Microsoft Sharepoint Portal Server 2003. Staff were trained on how to use the KM platform.

Today the KM programme is still running, staff share their knowledge based on the experiences, work and interest. When they face knowledge challenges in their work, staff members refer to the KM

---

platform to get ideas and insights. Different tools have been developed that not only encourage staff to share their knowledge through different channels but also enable them to identify the kinds of problems and solutions to find in the KM platform. The content of the platform is updated regularly to make it more user-friendly. There is also consideration of updating the KM platform to Microsoft Sharepoint Portal Server 2007.

KM strategies and tools in Youth Help:

Since Youth Help provides services requiring high human interaction with clients, its strategies are more people oriented. Some of the tools it is using are:

On line platform – the Microsoft Sharepoint Saver 2003 to ensure online knowledge sharing activities. It is used for official notices and upcoming events, for example; it can also upload documents to specific folders. There are several folders on the front page including personal sharing section, KM market and discussion forums.

Elicitation – a group discussion focusing on a particular issue. It is a facilitated session. The proceedings are documented and uploaded on the platform.

After action review – involves the process of note taking by someone observing the activity led, then noting down the strengths and weaknesses. Then the tacit knowledge is codified and uploaded.

Exit interview - the aim is to extract as much knowledge and experience from the members of staff who are leaving, so that this remains in the organization. The results are recorded and uploaded on the online platform for all to benefit from.

Statistical record - the top three staff who have logged in to the platform are rewarded with presents. They are also given other forms of recognition like being mentioned in a monthly newsletter.

Obstacles in implementing KM in Youth Help:

Youth Help has encountered a number of challenges in implementing its KM programme. Some of these are:

- Lack of KM background – the staff in Youth Help are development workers not KM professionals. Many of them have limited understanding or perhaps none at all of what KM is. This meant a lot of time spent in raising KM awareness and promoting it to become part of the culture of the organization.

- Delays – there were delays in implementing the KM strategy because there was a need to redesign the original organizational strategy, which had time and monetary implications.

- Lack of tailor made KM software; there was none of this for KM. They had to adapt existing software. Currently they are discussing with Microsoft designing of tailor made software for them.

- Lack of a formal team for the KM programme – Youth Help does not have a formal team to manage the whole KM programme. No one therefore takes responsibility for managing it.

- No organizational structure to provide follow up – there was no formal function in the organogram to handle the KM programme.

- Lack of resources – KM was not prioritized in the budget. Sometimes it was even forgotten.

Benefits of the KM programme:

Despite the above challenges, Youth Help derived some benefits from the KM programme:

- Benchmarking for the NGOs – Youth Help is seen as a leader among NGOs since they were the first to adapt KM as a practice.

- Getting positive feedback – the organization is more responsive as it gets feedback from the staff through the online platform.

- Facilitating the programme implementation process – the KM programme reduces the gaps between the plan and actual activities implemented, leading to efficiency in resource use.

How Modern Organizations Can Benefit from *Ubuntu* Learning and Knowledge Management Practices

From the above discussion, it can be observed that the practice of knowledge management in organizations is constrained by a number of challenges. These include:

- Inadequate knowledge and awareness of the concepts of learning and knowledge management, leading to less appreciation of the concept;

- Limited resources (time, money and commitment) allocated to organizational learning and knowledge management because it is not taken as a priority in many organizations;

- Inadequate reading and documentation skills;

- Lack of incentives and support for organizational learning and knowledge management;

- Physical distance, especially with field offices, and the fact that technology may not always replace physical human interaction;

- Organizational culture not receptive to organizational learning and knowledge management: 'Many organizations have implemented sophisticated intranets and other technologies while largely ignoring the complex cultural issues that influence the way people behave around knowledge...they implement state of the art technology and then discover that culture and behavior are slow to change.' Many organizations are too busy with *doing* at the expense of their *being*;

- Leadership not strong enough to sustain enthusiasm for organizational learning and knowledge management;

- Too much information, making it difficult to identify relevant and useful information;

- Pushing for results, making the intangible nature of learning and knowledge get less priority.

The practice of knowledge management and the lessons as described above can help modern organizations address some of the challenges listed above:

The information on the practice of knowledge management in *ubuntu* cultures can be used to raise awareness of the need for more effective organizational learning and knowledge practices in modern organizations.

In most organizations, knowledge management budgets (if they exist) are the first to be cut when the organization runs into difficult times. *Ubuntu* culture made learning and knowledge management an absolute necessity and could not imagine life without it.

Ubuntu cultures provided incentives to those individuals who showed distinction and excellence in learning. Proverbs such as *The child who washes his hands will eat with kings* illustrates the recognition that went to those individuals who demonstrated excellence in learning and knowledge management even if they were young in age.

Face to face meetings were prioritized. A meeting of minds and hearts, people believed, would be reached only through face to face meetings. This is why they would travel very long distances for such meetings even when it was possible to just send a message without having necessarily to go there. This means that while technologies that make meetings possible without having actually to meet physically may be important and efficient, they may not and should not replace the need for physical meetings. It is understood that these technologies will reduce the frequency of such meetings, but they should not replace them entirely. The other lesson is that the technologies can be used on 'efficiency' or not so deep issues, while face to face meetings must be reserved for deeper mind to mind and heart to heart communication and learning.

A key challenge in organizations today is too much information, making it difficult to identify relevant and useful information. *Ubuntu* cultures were concerned with only relevant and useful information. They concentrated on information and knowledge that helped them find ways to improve the life of the community. The emphasis was on what type of community they wanted to become and not so much on they already were. In other words organizational learning and knowledge management were driven by the communities' ideals of sharing and collective ownership of opportunities, responsibilities and challenges, the importance of people and relationships over things, participatory decision making and leadership, loyalty to the community, and reconciliation as a goal of conflict management. This concentration helped focus the learning and knowledge management and define what is useful knowledge and what is not.

Modern organizations are under pressure to meet deadlines and demonstrate impact. This causes learning and knowledge management to be pushed to the background. While *ubuntu* culture recognized the importance of results, it believed that *A healthy chick comes from a healthy egg* – and therefore concentrated on developing the *being* as the foundation for more effective *doing* and *relating*. Organizations cannot give in their *doing* and *relating* what they don't have in their *being*.

Another lesson from the *ubuntu* cultures is that learning by individuals was not meant to benefit only individuals but the entire community. In addition, learning was taken as a long-term if not lifelong process. The learning and knowledge management needs of the organization and the sectors are changing constantly, and so long-term and lifelong learning processes are necessary to adapt and implement change.

Conclusion

Effective knowledge management systems enable a conscious and integrated approach to identifying, creating, managing, sharing and making full use of all information and knowledge assets an organization has. It enables the organization to use its knowledge assets to create, compete and improve. This in turn will improve the organization's innovation, responsiveness and adaptability. Without an effective knowledge management strategy and system, the organization lacks organizational memory. Just like *The death of an elderly man is like burning an entire library*, the departure of key staff greatly undermines the organization's knowledge base.

To ensure effective knowledge management:

- Knowledge management must be guided by the organization we want to become (not what we already are). It must be based on the organization's ideal picture.

- The target for knowledge management is the internal stakeholders (staff and the board) rather than the people the organization serves. The aim of knowledge management is to create organizational intelligence that would enable the people in the organization to serve their beneficiaries better. The aim is to improve the organization's relevance, legitimacy and sustainability.

- The organization must agree on the most appropriate knowledge management tools for its situation. Young and small organizations need less and less complicated tools as compared to big and more established organizations.

- It is important to have an effective management plan that will enable everyone in the organization to buy into the knowledge management programme.

- It is important to think through at the beginning how the knowledge management initiative will be sustained; to think through the long-term requirements of money, time and energy.

In summary, kindling the organizational fire or learning and knowledge management involves reflecting and acting on: what the organization is learning from its practice, what it is learning from its relationships with its different stakeholders, what it is learning from changes in its task environment (political, economic, socio-cultural and technological factors), and how it is capturing, documenting and making accessible the lessons to all the staff and board members and making sure the lessons are being consciously used to improve performance. It is important for organizations to concentrate only on that knowledge that is critical to their success. This is because *Too much knowledge obscures wisdom.*

Reflection Proverbs

What can we learn about knowledge management in organizations from the following proverbs?

The people who cannot kindle their own fire are easy to defeat

Knowledge is like a baobab tree, no one person can embrace it alone

The death of an old person is like an entire library burnt

The palest ink is stronger than the strongest memory

A healthy chick comes from a healthy egg

Too much knowledge obscures wisdom

How can we use the lessons to improve knowledge management efforts in our organization?

APPENDICES:

SAMPLE DIAGNOSTIC INSTRUMENTS

Appendix 1

PROVERBS STRATEGIC THINKING SELF-ASSESSMENT TOOL

Rating (0 – 5): 0 = we do not experience this in our organization; 5 = we strongly experience or observe this in our organization

Strategic Thinking through African Proverbs

Rate yourself and explain why you give yourself that rate.

Rating (0 – 5): 0 = non – existent; 5 = excellent

1. How conscious is our organization of the importance of making lasting impact and leaving a strong legacy?

Everyone dies but not everyone lives.

All people die but not all are buried

Lions don't die, they just sleep

2. How well is the organization able to forecast possible future scenarios and plan on the basis of the scenarios?

You can only jump over a ditch if you can see it from afar

3. How well has our organization identified and strives to remain within its niche so that it maximizes its impact and minimizes competition?

A cat in his house has the teeth of a lion

4. How consciously has our organization made the following strategic decisions and adhered to them to ensure focus and concentration?

- Whether to be an implementer or facilitator.

- Whether to cover a large geographical area or to focus effort in a small area and expand gradually as we make impact.

- Whether to offer many projects/services or just a few.

- Whether to respond to root causes or symptoms (at what level of depth to intervene).

- Whether to work in isolation or in collaboration.

- Whether to take a short term or long term approach.

At the crossroads you cannot go in both directions at the same time

If you run after two hares, you will catch neither of them

5. How consciously does our organization pace the implementation of its strategy so that resources and capacity constraints do not become a bottleneck?

More haste less speed

No matter how hungry you are, you can only eat your meal one mouthful at a time

6. How regularly and consciously does our organization review its strategy to see if it is still relevant to the changing factors in the task environment?

When the beat of the drum changes so must the step of its dance

Appendix 2

PERSONAL DEVELOPMENT CONSCIOUSNESS SELF ASSESSMENT TOOL

Rate yourself and explain why you give yourself that rate.
Rate (0 – 5): 0 = non – existent; 5 = excellent

1. How conscious am I of the importance of personal or self-development?

The person who doesn't know where he is going will not get there

If a child washes his hands he will eat with kings

The greatest achievement is to master oneself

2. How clear is the vision and purpose of my life?

The eyes that have seen the sea cannot be satisfied by a mere lagoon

What the eyes have seen the heart cannot forget

3. How conscious am I about the importance of self-leadership?

It is better to be the head of a mouse than a tail of a lion

4. How conscious am I about who I am and my potential?

An eagle that does not know that it is an eagle lives like a chicken

It is better to fail with originality than succeed with imitation

5. How conscious am I about discovering my uniqueness and unique contribution to life?

Do not go where the path may lead, go instead where there is no path and leave a trail.

6. How conscious am I about the values and behaviour that I must embrace to
ensure the realization of my vision – accomplishment of my vision and mission?

The river that forgets its sources will soon dry up

If money grew on trees many people would be married to monkeys

•
7. How conscious am I of the contradictions in my values or behaviour that
would prevent me from realizing my vision and accomplishing my mission?

Many people smear themselves with mud and then complain that they are dirty

When you are pointing a finger of blame at someone the remaining four are pointing back at yourself

Judge each day not by its harvest but by the seeds you sow into it.

8. How conscious am I about the need to concentrate and focus my energy on a few key priority areas for impact and realization of my vision and mission?

The dog that belongs to everyone in the village will die of starvation

A hunter with one arrow does not shoot at careless aim

Rays of light concentrated through a lens can set an entire forest ablaze

9. How independent am I in my decision making and actions?

If two wise men agree on everything then there is no need for one of them

If you want your voice to be heard, simply talk

10. How conscious am I of the need for a mentor in my life and how well am I working with the mentor?

What old people see while seated, young people may not see standing on their toes

11. How well do I handle negative feedback from my mentor and other people in my life?

Because of lack of criticism, the warthog's teeth have grown disproportionately long

12. How careful am I about the choice of my mentor or source of advice?

Advice is like mushrooms, the wrong kind can be fatal

13. How well am I sequencing my steps with my journey towards personal development?

How conscious am I about the need for patience in the journey towards self-mastery?

Take it easy with the drum, the night is still long

Short cuts are full of mud

A patient mouse in a young banana plant will one day eat a ripe banana

The journey of a thousand miles starts with one step

14. How conscious am I about my limitations and the need to work with them rather than against them?

The dry grass should not challenge the fire

It was ignorance that made the rat challenge the cat to a wrestling match

It is a stupid dog that barks at an elephant

What business does an egg have dancing with the stones?

15. How well do I manage obstacles, challenges and setbacks in my journey of
personal development?

A person is taller than any mountain they have climbed

16. How well and fast do I carry out my intentions and resolutions?

Good intentions are like babies crying in church, they should be carried out immediately

Ideas are like a baby, easy to conceive but difficult to deliver

Don't tell people what you will do; show them what you have done

Appendix 3

SOME ORGANIZATIONAL AND KNOWLEDGE
MANAGEMENT TOOLS

Tool 1: Peer assists

The peer assists tool supports 'learning before doing' processes. It begins with the premise that for any given activity, someone else has done something before that is at least broadly similar. First identify the right group of people and use a systematic method to benefit from their insights and experience. Peer assists promote learning and can be used to strengthen mutual learning between people and groups in the organization.

Steps:

- Develop a clear definition of the problem or issue to be addressed.

- Enlist participants through open invitation or selection.

- Time the meeting carefully to ensure enough notice time for participants and their availability and ensure that the lessons can be used effectively by the people needing the peer assist.

Tool 2: Challenge sessions

Many people assume that the future will just be an extension of the past and the present. They are not comfortable with the idea that the future might be radically different from the known past and present and might therefore require new knowledge and behaviour from us. Accepting the possibility of a radically different future makes it easier to adjust to the new implied demands.

Challenge session is a tool that helps to develop capacity to create change in the way that groups and individuals think and solve problems, especially as these relate to the future. The basis of a challenge session is to generate a series of challenge statements, defined as deliberately provocative statements about a particular situation. The aim is to generate ideas; people move away from conventional modes of thinking and provide a starting point for original, creative thinking. An example could be – let's assume our funding has been halved or let's assume we will lose 50% of our professional staff over the next one year.

The process is as follows:

Identify the problem: this should be a well defined problem or issue faced by the team or organization.

Brainstorm a series of challenge statements, like the ones above; this may be done with the whole group or sub groups.

Use the challenge statements to generate new ideas: address the following checklist:

- What are the consequences of the statement?
- What are the possible opportunities and threats implied by the consequences?
- What are the principles needed to take advantage of the opportunities and address the threats?
- How would it work in a step by step process?
- What would happen if the sequence of events was changed?
- Prioritize the ideas, use pilots to test the ideas and then roll out widely.

As with good lateral thinking techniques, use of challenge sessions does not guarantee production of good and relevant ideas, though it can help generate completely new ideas and concepts. The key is effective facilitation of the group through a creative thinking process.

Tool 3: After Action Review

After action review is a simple tool that enables continuous assessment of organizational performance looking at successes and failures, ensuring that learning takes place to support continuous improvement. It works by bringing together a team to discuss tasks, events, activities or projects in an open and honest fashion. A systematic approach of this tool is crucial in driving organizational change. It is the key aspect for organizational learning and motivation.

Description

The essence is to bring together the relevant group to think about a project, activity, event or task and pose the following questions:

Question	Purpose
What was supposed to happen? What actually happened? Why were there discrepancies?	These questions establish a common understanding of the work item under review. Differences from plans should especially be explored.
What worked well? Why? What did not work well? Why?	These questions generate reflection about success and failures during the course of the project, activity, event or task. The question 'why' generates understanding of the root causes of these successes and failures
What would you do differently next time?	This question is intended to help identify specific actionable recommendations. They must be crisp and clear and achievable and future oriented

Tool 4: Intranet strategies

Intranets play a critical role in knowledge management. They need however to be applied carefully and in response to clearly specified needs. There needs to be clear cut reasons and a supporting strategy for the intranet deployed in the organization, otherwise information posted will not be continually updated or accessed. Intranets should also not be seen as silver bullets to slay all organizational KM problems in the organization.

There are three potential benefits of intranets in organizations. These are:

- Information collection
- Collaboration and communication
- Task completion

While it is clear that no intranet will focus on only one of these applications, most successful intranets have a priority focus on one approach, with others playing a supportive role. This needs to be determined by the overall organizational strategy for knowledge and learning, and each has different resource implications.

Description of the process:

Information collection: intranets are used to find and organize all of the information that resides within the organization, essentially acting as a front end to a large repository of knowledge. There could be document libraries, individuals' computer files, financial and statistical data, supplier information, databases, organizational policies, systems and procedures and other information that was previously only available to selected people or groups within the organization. Access to this information reduces confusion and duplication, increases productivity and improves decision making. In a system wholly geared towards information collection, individuals contribute and have access to a wealth of information but do not use the system to interact with other contributors.

Collaboration and communication – intranets enable organizational units to connect with others within the organization, and to initiate and participate in essential information flows. In contrast to information collection intranet, collaboration and communication intranet promotes dialogue, debate, learning and help to facilitate face to face communications. It also helps in situations where face to face interactions are made difficult because of physical distance. Typical features might include discussion forums, internal bulletins, surveys, organizational calendars, and question and answer facilities.

Activity based intranets facilitate the completion of tasks and actions. For example the intranet may be used to reserve rooms, raise purchases, change human resource information, fill out and submit timesheets, purchase supplies and complete necessary forms. This kind of system reduces the time spent on often repeated administrative tasks and increases the time available for core business.

There are nine critical factors to ensure success in use of intranets. These are:

- Develop a two- to three-year intranet strategy, based on considerations of content, process requirements, technology and other resources, and governance mechanisms. This strategy should include a clear set of objectives for the intranet which are monitored and regularly reviewed.

- Match information on the intranet to the business needs – the intranet needs to match existing and future organizational needs and not just be a random collection of information. Establish an appropriate balance between information collection, collaboration and communication; and task completion approaches.

- Obtain a sponsor – ensure there is a senior management champion and that this person has budget control. Without this sponsorship the intranet will not be seen as an organization-wide tool and will not have sufficient resources allocated to it.

- Recognize authorship – the roles, skills and responsibilities for contribution and maintenance should be included in job descriptions and reviews. Intranet contribution is not a hobby but should be rewarded and recognized.

- Provide access to the external environment – the intranet should provide access to external information such as donor and partner information, funding information, research websites, databases etc.

- Develop clear information architecture – this should be as simple and as easy to communicate as possible and ideally should not replicate the existing organizational structure. A clear thematic and information type taxonomy should be applied.

- Undertake regular usability testing – there should be regular and systematic feedback loops from users to ensure that information and the system as a whole meet changing user needs.

- Establish a marketing strategy – to promote the intranet and its use among all staff. This must focus not only on new information but on how the tool can be applied in day to day work.

- Assess impact – the performance of the intranet needs to be measured against objectives, using surveys, success stories and failure stories.

Tool 5: Exit interview

Increasingly exit interviews are being viewed as rare learning opportunities as they are meant to minimize the loss of useful knowledge through staff turnover. The leaver gets to reflect on their role and, it is hoped, depart on a positive note leaving a positive impact on the organization. Conducting exit interviews can also be highly therapeutic, especially for staff who are leaving volatile environments.

Process

The ideal focus of the learning based exit interview is on knowledge that is most useful to the next person or for others doing similar work in the organization. It must be arranged as early as possible when it is known that the person will be leaving.

- Identify who in the organization might benefit and what they need to know from the person who is leaving. Think about the explicit and tacit knowledge that needs to be explained.

143

- Develop a plan in a participatory way to ensure knowledge can be captured and documented during the leaver's notice period. This requires a review of key tasks, drawing from a TOR consultation with the leaving staff. For explicit knowledge the leaver should move relevant files – hard and electronic – into a shared folder or a document library and prepare handover notes for the successor.

Tool 6: How to Guides

How to guides enable the know-how of some staff within the organization to be captured, documented and made available to others. This ensures that the knowledge is available to the whole organization. Useful how to guides might: 1. be related to programming and projects, e.g. community development, gender and HIV and AIDS; 2. contain knowledge about a relationship with a particular type of a stakeholder, e.g. donors; 3. give knowledge about a key system, technology or piece of equipment, e.g. how to access intranet while travelling; 5. provide knowledge about organizational culture and internal infrastructure.

To ensure success think about the purpose, understand the audience, find knowledgeable sources, choose appropriate researchers and the right questions, organize package and share, evaluate and adapt.

Tool 7: Staff profile pages

Organizational staff profile pages are electronic directories with information about staff in the organization. In addition to information on most staff profiles, these contain details about knowledge, skills, experiences, interests and even hobbies of staff with the aim of facilitating knowledge and learning initiatives and linking like-minded people for collaboration opportunities.

Staff Profile Page

> Job title:
>
> Department or team:
>
> Photograph:
>
> Contact information:
>
> A brief job description:
>
> Current and previous projects:
>
> Trip reports:
>
> Areas of current knowledge and experience:
>
> Areas of interest;
>
> Countries of interest:
>
> Key contacts – both internal and external e.g. key donors, valuable partners:
>
> Membership to local and international networks:
>
> Relevant professional qualifications:
>
> Personal profile: hobbies, interests, birthday e.t.c.
>
> An updated CV (multiple versions possible):

Tool 8: The Knowledge Management Assessment Tool (KMAT)

This tool is adapted from the knowledge management tool (KMAT) developed by the American Productivity of Quality Centre and Arthur Andersen in 1995. The tool helps organizations to self-assess where the strengths and opportunities lie in managing knowledge in the organization.

The tool is divided into five sections: the KM process; leadership; culture; technology; measurement. The following is a subset of the items and information in the KMAT, with a simplified scoring system.

Instruction: Read the statements below and evaluate your organization's performance. The scale is as follows:

1= no, 2 = poor, 3 = fair, 4 = good and 5 = excellent

I. The Knowledge Management Process

P1. Knowledge gaps are systematically identified and well-defined processes are used to close them.

-1 -2 -3 -4 -5

Comments: ....
....

P2. A sophisticated and professional knowledge gathering mechanism has been developed

-1 -2 -3 -4 -5

Comments: ....
....

P3. All members of the organization are involved in looking for ideas (in traditional and non-traditional places) to improve the organization's performance.

-1 -2 -3 -4 -5

Comments: ....
....

P4. The organization has formalized the process of transferring best practices, including documentation and lessons learnt

-1 -2 -3 -4 -5

Comments: ....
....

P5. 'Tacit' knowledge (what employees know how to do, but cannot or do not express) is valued and transferred across the organization

-1 -2 -3 -4 -5

Comments: ....
....

P6. A conscious system is in place to ensure that the new knowledge gathered is integrated into practice

-1 -2 -3 -4 -5

Comments:..

....

Total for items P1 – P6:

II. Leadership in Knowledge Management

L1. Managing organizational knowledge is central to the organization's strategic plan

-1 -2 -3 -4 -5

Comments:..

....

L2. The organization understands the critical role of its knowledge assets in its financial and organizational sustainability and develops strategies for marketing and selling them

-1 -2 -3 -4 -5

Comments:..

....

L3. The organization consciously uses organizational learning to support existing core competencies and create new ones

-1 -2 -3 -4 -5

Comments:..

....

L4. An individual's contribution to the development of organizational knowledge plays a critical role in the organization's hiring, appraisal and compensation or remuneration practices.

-1 -2 -3 -4 -5

Comments:..

....

Total for items L1 – L4:

III. *Knowledge Management Culture*

C1. The organization encourages and facilitates knowledge sharing
-1 -2 -3 -4 -5
Comments:...
....
....

C2. A climate of openness and trust permeates the organization
-1 -2 -3 -4 -5
Comments:...
....
....

C3. Creating value for beneficiaries is acknowledged as a major
objective of knowledge management
-1 -2 -3 -4 -5
Comments:...
....
....

C4. Flexibility and a desire to innovate (and allowing people to make
mistakes in the process as long as they can learn from them) drive the
learning process in the organization
-1 -2 -3 -4 -5
Comments:...
....
....

C5. Employees take responsibility for their own learning rather than
waiting for the organization to provide all learning opportunities.
-1 -2 -3 -4 -5
Comments:...
....
....

Total for items C1 through C5:

IV. Knowledge Management Technology

T1. Technology for knowledge management in the organization links all staff members to one another and to all relevant external publics
-1 -2 -3 -4 -5
Comments: ....
....
....

T2. Technology in the organization creates an institutional memory that is accessible to the entire organization
-1 -2 -3 -4 -5
Comments: ....
....
....

T3. Technology for knowledge management brings the organization closer to its beneficiaries
-1 -5 -3 -4 -5
Comments: ....
....
....

T4. The organization fosters the development of 'client-centred' information technology
-1 -2 -3 -4 -5
Comments: ....
....
....

T5. Technology that supports intra-organizational collaboration is rapidly placed in the hands of staff
-1 -2 -3 -4 -5
Comments: ....
....
....

T6. Information systems in the organization are integrated and specific, measurable, achievable,
   realistic and time-bound (SMART)
   -1 -2 -3 -4 -5
   Comments: ....
   ....
   ....

Total for T1 – T6:

V. Knowledge Management Measurement

M1. The organization has invented ways to link knowledge to development results
   -1 -2 -3 -4 -5
   Comments: ....
   ....
   ....

M2. The organization has developed a specific set of indicators to manage knowledge
   -1 -2 -3 -4 -5
   Comments: ....
   ....
   ....

M3. The organization's set of indicators on knowledge management balances hard and soft as well as financial and non-financial measures
   -1 -2 -3 -4 -5
   Comments: ....
   ....
   ....

M4. The organization allocates resources towards efforts that consciously and measurably increase its knowledge base
   -1 -2 -3 -4 -5
   Comments: ....
   ....
   ....

Total of items M1 through M4:

REFERENCES

Associated Press, 2008. 'Honey Bee Crisis Could Lead to Higher Food Prices', 28.06.08.

Bennis, W. and R. Thomas, 2002. *Geeks and Geezers: How Era, Values and Defining Moments Shape Leaders*. Harvard Business School Press, Boston, MA.

Brocke-Utne, B., 2001. 'Indigenous Conflict Resolution in Africa', Paper Presented to the Weekend Seminar on Indigenous Solutions to Conflicts held at the University of Oslo, Institute for Educational Research, 23-24 February 2001.

Buber, M., 1937. *I and Thou*. T & T Clark, Edinburgh.

Bulhungu, S., 1999. 'Generational Transition in Union Unemployment: Organizational Implications for Staff Turnover.' *Transformation – Critical Perspectives* 39 (1999): 47-71.

Chadha, P., A. Jaganada and G. Lal, 2003. *Organizational Behavior for Non-Governmental Development Organizations*. Bhunanswar: Center for Youths and Social Development.

Chartered Institute of Personnel and Development, 2008. *Leadership and Management of Conflict at Work*. London: CIPD.

Church, M., 200.) 'Participation, Relationships and Dynamic Change: New Thinking on Evaluating the Work of International Workshops', DPU UCL, Working Paper 121: London.

Cohen, D., R. Vega and G. Watson, 2001. *Advocacy for Social Justice: A Global Action and Reflection Guide* Kumarian Press: Bloomfield, USA.

Cole, G., 1997. *Personnel Management: Theory and Practice*. Continuum, London.

Conger, J., 1989. *The Charismatic Leader: Behind the Mystique of Exceptional Leadership*. Jossey-Bass Publishers, San Francisco

Covey, S., 2004. *The 8th Habit: From Effectiveness to Greatness*. Simon & Schuster, London

Dainty, P. and M. Anderson, 1996. *The Capable Executive: Effective Performance in Senior Management.* Macmillan Press Ltd, London.

Drucker, P., 1955. *Managing for Results.* Butterworth-Heinemann, Oxford.

Drucker, P., 1967. *The Effective Executive.* Butterworth-Heinemann, Oxford.

Drucker, P., 1974. *Management: Tasks, Responsibilities, Practices.* Butterworth-Heinemann, Oxford.

Drucker, P., 1980. *Managing in Turbulent Times.* Butterworth-Heinemann, Oxford.

Drucker, P., 1990. *Managing the Non-Profit Organisation.* Butterworth -Heinemann, Oxford.

Drucker, P., 1991. *Managing for the Future.* Butterworth-Heinemann, Oxford.

Dunphy, D., 1981. *Organisational Change by Choice.* McGraw-Hill Book Company, Auckland.

Foot, M. and C. Hook, 1999. *Introducing Human Resource Management.* London: Prentice Hall.

Fowler, A. (2001). 'A Guide to Good Governance of NGOs.' *NGO Leadership Development Series no 1.* Nairobi: Kenya Council of NGOs.

French, W. and C. Bell Jnr, 1995. *Organization Development: Behavioural Science Interventions for Organisation Improvement (5th edition).* Prentice-Hall Inc, New Jersey.

Hammer, M., 2003. *The Agenda: What Every Business Must Do to Dominate the Decade.* Three Rivers: New York.

Hammer, M. and J. Champy, 2001. *Reengineering the Corporation,* Nicholas Brealey Publishing, London.

Hamylin, J., 1996. 'Halt Labor Turnover', *Information Technology Review* 3(1), 42-6.

Handy, C., 1985. *Understanding Organisations.* Penguin Group, London.

Handy, C., 1998. *Understanding Voluntary Organisations.* Penguin, Harmondsworth.

Handy, C., 2006. *Myself and Other More Important Matters.* Arrow Books, Croydon, Surrey.

Hanson, P, and B. Lubin, 1995. *Answers to Questions most Frequently Asked About Organisation Development.* Sage Publications, London.

Harvard Business Review, 2006. *Classic Drucker: Essential Wisdom of Peter Drucker from the Pages of Harvard Business Review,* Harvard Business School Publishing Corporation, Boston, MA.

Herman, S., 2001. 'Notes on OD for the 21st Century Organisation', *Organisation Development Journal* Vol 19 No 1.

Holloway, R., 1997. *Exit Strategies: Transition from International to Local NGO Leadership,* PACT, Washington DC.

Jackson, D., 1997. *Dynamic Organisations: The Challenge of Change.* Macmillan Press Ltd, London.

Jackson, T., 2002. *Theories in Management and Change in Africa.* www.Africamgt.org

James, R., 1998. *Demystifying Organisation Development: Practical Capacity Building Experience of African NGOs,* INTRAC, Oxford.

James, R., 2002. *People and Change: Exploring Capacity Building in NGOs.* INTRAC, Oxford.

James, R., 2003. 'Leaders Changing Inside-Out: What Causes Leaders to Change Behaviour? Cases from Malawian Civil Society.' The International NGO Training and Research Centre INTRAC Occasional Papers Series No. 43.

James, R. and C. Malunga, 2006. 'Organizational Challenges Facing Civil Society Networks in Malawi', *KM4D Journal* 2 (2): 48-63.

Johnson, H. and G. Wilson, 1999. 'Institutional Sustainability as Learning', *Development in Practice* Vol 9 no 1 & 2.

Kaplan, A., 1996. *The Development Practitioners' Handbook.* Pluto Press, London.

Kaplan, A., 1999. *The Development of Capacity.* Washington: NGLS

Kemp, R., 1990. 'The Need for Strategic Planning in the Public and Non-Profit Sector', *People* 24: 15-17.

Kriesberg, L., 2001. 'Changing Forms of Co-existence' in M. Abu-Nimer (Ed.), *Reconciliation, Justice and Co-existence: Theory and Practice*, Lexington Books, Lanham, ML.

Kumakanga, S., 1975. *Nzeru za Kale (Wisdom of Ancient Times)*, Longman, Blantyre.

Lebow, R. and W. Simon, 1997. *Lasting Change: The Shared Values Process that Makes Companies Great.* John Wiley & Sons, Inc., New York.

Lettieri, E., F. Borga, and A. Savoldelli, 2004. 'Knowledge Management in Non Profit Organizations', *Journal of Knowledge Management* Vol 8 Issue 6, pp 16-30.

Levinson, M., 2008. *ABC: An Introduction to Knowledge Management (KM).* New Jersey: CIO.

Livegoed, B., 1969. *Managing the Developing Organisation.* Blackwell, Oxford.

Livegoed, B., 1973. *The Developing Organisation.* Tavistock, London.

Lynch, J., 1995. *Customer Loyalty and Success.* Macmillan Press Ltd, London.

Madden, T., 1986. 'Joking Relationships', *Journal of the Royal College of General Practitioners*, May 1986.

Malunga, C., 2000. 'The Beehive Model for Team Building', Paper Published in *Footsteps Magazine* no 4.

Malunga, C., 2003. 'An Investigation into Factors Affecting Staff Turnover amongst Professional Staff in NGO's in Malawi', Master's Dissertation, University of South Africa.

Malunga, C, 2004. *Understanding Organizational Sustainability through African Proverbs.* Impact Alliance, Washington DC.

Malunga, C., 2007. 'Improving the Effectiveness of Strategic Planning in NGOs in Malawi', PhD Thesis, University of South Africa.

Mandela, N., 1994. *Long Walk to Freedom*. Little, Brown and Co., London.

Mapadimeng, M., 2007. 'Ubuntu/botho, the Work Place and the 'Two Economies'', *Journal of Development Studies*, Vol 37 No 2.

Mbeki, T., 1998. *The African Renaissance: South Africa and the World*. United Nations University, Tokyo.

Mbigi, L., 1995. Ubuntu – *The Spirit of African Transformation Management*. Knowledge Resource, Randburg.

Megginson, D. and M. Peddler, 1992. *Self-Development: A Facilitator's Guide*. McGraw-Hill Book Company, Berkshire.

Miller, P., 2005. 'The Rise of Network Campaigning', in H. McCarthy, P. Miller and P. Skidmore (Eds), 'Network Logic: Who Governs in an Interconnected World?' www.demos.co.uk/catalogue/networks-page 404.aspx.Demos

Molotlegi, K., 2004. 'Indigenous Leadership for Progressing Africa', Paper Presented on 12 October 2004 in Addis Ababa.

Morgan, G., 1989. *Images of Organisation*. Sage Publications, London.

Morgan, G., 1997. *Imaginization: New Mindsets for Seeing, Organizing, and Managing*. Sage Publications, London.

Mulle, H., 2001. 'Challenges to African Governance and Civil Society', *Public Administration and Development* Vol 21, pp 71-6.

Munroe, M., 1996. *Maximising Your Potential: The Keys to Dying Empty*, Destiny Image Publishers, Inc, Shippensburg.

Murithi, T. n.d. 'Practical Peace Making Wisdom from Africa: Reflections on ubuntu.' www.bath,ac.uk

Murithi, T. 2006. 'Practical Peacemaking Wisdom from Africa: Reflections on Ubuntu', *The Journal of Pan African Studies*, vol 1 no 4, June 2006.

Nangoli, M., 1986. *No More Lies about Africa: Here's the Truth from an African*, Heritage Publishers, New Jersey.

Natemeyer, W., 1979. *Situational Leadership, Perception, and the Impact of Power*. Escondido, CA: Leadership Studies.

National Center for Non Profit Boards, 2000. 'Critical Components of Effective Governance: A Regional Training of Trainers Course Designed for Non Profit Organizations of Southern Africa', Johannesburg, 30 May 30-2 June 2000.

Nchabeleng, L., 2000. 'Making Change: A Challenge to Leaders in the Leaders in the New Millenium', *OD Debate* 7 (3): 4-7.

Nonaka, I., 1998. 'The Concept of 'Ba': Building Foundation for Knowledge Creation', *California Management Review* vol 40 no 3, Spring 1998.

Olive Subscription Service, 1997. *How Well Do You Read Your Organisation? Ideas for a Change.* Olive Publications, Durban.

Parker, M., 1990. *Team Players and Team Work: The New Competitive Business Strategy.* Jossey-Bass, San Francisco.

Poovan, N., M.K. du Toit and A. Engelbrecht, 2006. 'The Effect of Social Values of Ubuntu on Team Effectiveness', *South African Journal of Business Management*, 2006, 37 (3).

Porter, L. and S. Tanner, 1998. *Assessing Business Excellence.* Butterworth-Heinemann, Oxford.

Raven, B., 1959. 'The Bases of Social Power', in D. Cartwright (Ed), *Studies in Social Power* (pp. 15-67). Institute for Social Research, University of Michigan, Ann Arbor, MI.

Sampson, A., 1999. *Mandela: The Authorised Biography.* HarperCollins Publishers, London.

Sahley, C., 1995. *Strengthening the Capacity of NGOs: Cases of Small Enterprises Development in Africa.* INTRAC, Oxford.

Senge, P., 1990. *The Fifth Discipline: The Art and Practice of the Learning Organisation,* Doubleday, New York.

Senge, P., C. Scharmer, J. Jaworski and B. Flowers, 2004. *Presence: Human Purpose and the Field of the Future.* Society for Organisational Learning, Inc, Cambridge, MA.

Smillie, I, and J. Hailley, 2001. *Managing for Change: Leadership, Strategy and Management in Asian NGOs.* Earthscan Publications Ltd, London.

Stewart, D., 2005. *Wisdom from Africa: A Collection of Proverbs*. Struik Publishers, Cape Town.

Suzuki, N., 1998. *Inside NGOs: Learning to Manage Conflicts between Headquarters and Field Offices*. London: Intermediate Technology Publishers

Tandon, R., 1995. 'Board Games-Governance: Governance and Accountability in NGOs,' in *Non Governmental Organizations – Performance and Accountability: Beyond the Magic Bullet*. Earthscan, London.

Tandon, R., 1996. *Understanding Design of Organisation*. PRIA, New Delhi, WA: Kola Tree Productions.

Taylor, 2001. 'CABUNGO Evaluation: Developing NGOs in Malawi.' Unpublished CABUNGO Report, Blantyre.

Tear Fund, 2003. *Peace Building within Our Communities*. Tear Fund, London.

Tengey, W., 1991. *A Guide to Promote Rural Self-Reliant Development (a Ghana Experience)*. Africa Centre for Human Development, Accra.

Thaw, D., 1999. *Developing Policy for Organisations: an Organic Process*. Olive Publications, Durban.

Tutu, D., 1999. *No Future Without Forgiveness*. Rider Books, London.

Vincent, F., 1995. *Alternative Financing of Third World Development Organisations and NGOs*, IRED, Geneva.

Waiguchu, J., 2001. *Management of Organisations in Africa: A Handbook and Reference*. Quorum Books, London.

Weisz, P., 1967. *The Science of Biology*, McGraw Hill Book Company. New York.

Williams, A., 2002. 'On the Subject of Kings and Queens: "Indigenous African Leadership and the Diasporal Imagination".' African Studies Quarterly/ www.africa.uf/.edu/ asq/v7:a4.htm

INDEX